D0200564

Everything You Know About Love and Sex Is Wrong

♥

ALSO BY PEPPER SCHWARTZ, Ph.D.

The Great Sex Weekend (with Janet Lever)

201 Questions to Ask Your Parents/
201 Questions to Ask Your Kids

The Love Test (with Virginia Rutter)

What I Learned About Sex (with Debra Haffner)

The Gender of Sexuality (with Virginia Rutter)

Love Between Equals: What Peer Marriage Really Means

American Couples: Money, Work, and Sex
(with Philip Blumstein)

Women at Yale (with Janet Lever)

Pepper Schwartz, Ph.D.

G. P. PUTNAM'S SONS
NEW YORK

Everything You Know About Love and Sex Is Wrong

Twenty-five
Relationship
Myths Redefined
to Achieve
Happiness and
Fulfillment
in Your
Intimate Life

Except for the personal experiences of the author, all cases and characters in this book are composites from acquaintances and clinical work. Names and details have been changed to protect privacy and confidentiality. This book is not intended as a substitute for advice from a trained counselor, therapist, or other mental health professional. If you are currently in counseling or therapy, check with your mental health provider before altering or discontinuing your therapeutic regimen.

G. P. Putnam's Sons
Publishers Since 1838
a member of
Penguin Putnam Inc.
375 Hudson Street
New York, NY 10014

Copyright © 2000 by Pepper Schwartz, Ph.D.
All rights reserved. This book, or parts thereof, may not
be reproduced in any form without permission.
Published simultaneoulsy in Canada

Library of Congress Cataloging-in-Publication Data

Schwartz, Pepper.
Everything you know about love and sex is wrong : twenty-five
relationship myths redefined to achieve happiness and fulfillment
in your intimate life / by Pepper Schwartz.
p.   cm.
ISBN 0-399-14655-5
1. Man-woman relationships.   2. Love.   3. Sex.   4. Mate selection.   I. Title.
HQ801.S4398   2000   00-039157
306.7—dc21

Printed in the United States of America
10   9   8   7   6   5   4   3   2   1

This book is printed on acid-free paper. ∞

BOOK DESIGN BY AMANDA DEWEY

Acknowledgments

Many people help a book be born. First of all I would like to thank Jim Becker and Andy Mayer for giving me the idea for this book—and for general good times and great brainstorming. Several people in their publishing/packaging house have laid hands on this book, and some of their names escape me—for which I apologize. But I do want to thank Kerry Tessaro, Suzanne De Galan, and Maggie Stanphill, who helped herd this book to its destination.

I am, as usual, indebted to all the good people at Perigee/Putnam, especially my editor, Jennifer Repo, and publisher John Duff. And I want to thank all the people who gave me good ideas for myths—including my friends on a women's trade misson to Eastern Europe who gave me great ideas: Constance Rice, Leslie Jones, Dorothy Mann, and Bernie Dochtal.

My husband, Art Skolnik, was supportive as always—and in this case extra supportive when I went away for almost three weeks and hid until most of this book was written. My kids, Cooper Schwartz Skolnik and Ryder Schwartz Skolnik, also could not have been more generous about giving me up so that the book could be written. All three are much loved and thanked for their graciousness and goodwill.

This book gets a special thanks and dedication to my friends Gail Sage Damazo and Ray Damazo, who, unasked, offered me the solitude and magnificence of their country estate in Rutland, England. My days at Burley on the Hill and Oakham will always be a highlight of my life. They allowed me a kind of discipline and isolation that made the book better—and certainly helped me complete it a lot sooner. People who are privileged enough to know Ray and Gail and be included in their hospitality and generosity know that being a friend of theirs is a special gift in life.

No one, of course, is responsible for the opinions and advice in this book except me. I am sure some of my dearest friends, colleagues, and family disagree with parts of it. I look forward to many heated and delightful conversations with them about this book—and hope some of these conversations will include you, the reader for whom this book has been written.

Contents

Introduction   *1*

1 ♥ Myth: Your lover should be your best friend   *5*

2 ♥ Myth: You can't be in love with two people at the same time   *15*

3 ♥ Myth: You will know when you have met "the one"   *27*

4 ♥ Myth: Pick only someone you are madly in love with   *39*

5 ♥ Myth: When you want to get serious, date only people with marriage potential   *49*

6 ♥ Myth: You should be similar to your partner   *59*

7 ♥ Myth: Pick someone who has sown her or his wild oats and is now ready to settle down with you   *73*

8 ♥ Myth: It is flattering to have a jealous lover   *79*

9 ♥ Myth: You should never have sex on the first date   *89*

10 ♥ Myth: Even if sex isn't fantastic in the beginning, it can be fixed   *101*

11 ♥ Myth: Masturbation by a partner in a relationship is a bad sign   *113*

12 ♥ Myth: Women are not into sex toys, pornography,
fantasy, or quickies   *123*

13 ♥ Myth: Men are simply not monogamous by nature; women are   *133*

14 ♥ Myth: You can't have really great sex without intercourse   *143*

15 ♥ Myth: If you desire someone else, something is wrong
with your relationship   *155*

16 ♥ Myth: Never go to bed mad   *163*

17 ♥ Myth: You can never truly get over even one act of infidelity   *173*

18 ♥ Myth: You should be prepared to do anything for
the person you love   *183*

19 ♥ Myth: Little annoying habits are unimportant
in a long-term relationship   *195*

20 ♥ Myth: Everyone should cohabit before marriage; it can only help   *209*

21 ♥ Myth: All committed couples (and especially spouses)
should pool their money   *221*

22 ♥ Myth: You should always be one hundred percent honest
with your partner   *231*

23 ♥ Myth: Divorce means failure; marriage should last a lifetime   *245*

24 ♥ Myth: Children bring a couple closer   *257*

25 ♥ Myth: Committed and married people should
live in the same home   *267*

Some concluding remarks   *275*

Introduction

This book is based on the proposition that a lot of popularly held assumptions about love and sex are just that: *assumptions.* We have been told some things so often we just assume they are true rather than think, "*Maybe* these rules aren't true, or perhaps more to the point, maybe they aren't true *for me.*" It is hard to think originally about how to have a relationship when certain models have been held up to us as tried-and-true our whole life. That's why, even when these models don't seem to be right for us, or are out and out failing us, we still try to do things the old way even when those ways are obviously not working for us.

I want to help you take a fresh look at a whole lot of sacred cows. And if some of what I say makes a lot of sense, don't feel embarrassed that you have never reconsidered some of these assumptions. We all have talked to friends, read magazine articles and survey results, we remember what our mothers told us, and by the time we're adults in long-term, committed relationships (or looking for one), we've absorbed this "wisdom" to the point that it's virtually unconscious. We don't question what we understand to be "facts." And that means that, intentionally or not, we force ourselves and our partners to adhere to certain rules or behavior that we believe to be irrefutable—even if they are not.

As a researcher, professor, journalist, and advice columnist I have talked to thousands of women and men whose search to find and keep a life partner is guided by "golden rules" that are nothing of the sort. I read the same advice that they do and I know where they get their guidelines. But I know that some of this advice is just not right, because of a person's particular background, personality, age, or goals. So I want to help people think "out of the box" and with a more practical than politically correct approach. In this book I take on the cherished myths that may be actually undermining us, and show why we hold on to these ideas and why we should let go of them.

The information in this book is backed up by knowledge of both clinical and research studies, and a more-than-twenty-five-year career as a sociology professor at the University of Washington in Seattle. But I get insights from other places as well. Certainly, I get them from my own life. I lived the sixties and seventies with enthusiasm, have been married twice, and have two teenagers and two stepchildren—all of which has taught me a lot. But some of my insights in this book are just from people I know well or people who have confided in me about their love and sex life and who, over time, have shown me that there is far more than one way to answer a relationship question satisfactorily. I have seen people come up with unique—and excellent—solutions to the two greatest questions of life: How can I love and be loved? How can I be happy and make someone else happy?

♥

The book takes on twenty-five ideas that I think are important, twenty-five myths that, if swallowed whole, could be fatal for some people's happiness and relationships. That doesn't mean that the things

I suggest are perfectly good guidelines for everyone, either. But I hope that you will be able to get enough out of each chapter to see if this is an area where you might benefit from some rethinking. I include some discussion of why we have believed this statement to be true, why it isn't always (or ever) true, and a few suggestions about what to do instead. What I don't do is harp on something I hope you will keep in your mind all the time: that your first obligation to yourself is to be healthy and safe. This isn't a book about contraceptive safety, and I don't dwell on the darker side of dating or relationships. But that doesn't mean that I don't recognize the many thoughts about "It won't be me" or "He won't ever hit me again" that rightly concern men and women in the dating market or in relationships. Please take care of yourself— know that some of my suggestions mean even greater attention to safer sex practices and that for the purposes of this book, I am assuming that you know that the only answer to any real verbal or physical abuse from a partner is a quick exit.

So let's look at the topics I do consider. I know some of these are controversial, but please try to overcome the knee-jerk reaction of telling me to go to hell and give them a little consideration. I might write these up with a sense of humor—but I believe deeply in what I'm saying. And I am truly hoping that at least a few of the ideas in this book will help spare you some real misery. If they do, let me hear from you. And even better—if you have a few of your own observations about what is a myth, I'd like to know them. I think the more myths we put to bed, the better. Life is tough enough. We don't need to feed ourselves lies (or unwittingly tell them to others). We need to get real, know what relationships really require, and find the solution that is fitted to who we are, rather than a one-size-fits-all approach. Intuitively we know that blanket prescriptions for love and sex can't be right. We are far too quirky and opinionated to feel there is only one way to conduct our sexual and emotional life. Listen to your inner voice, and you will connect with a lot of the things that I am saying. Not everything, of course, but enough to reshape your intimate life in a way that suits you better.

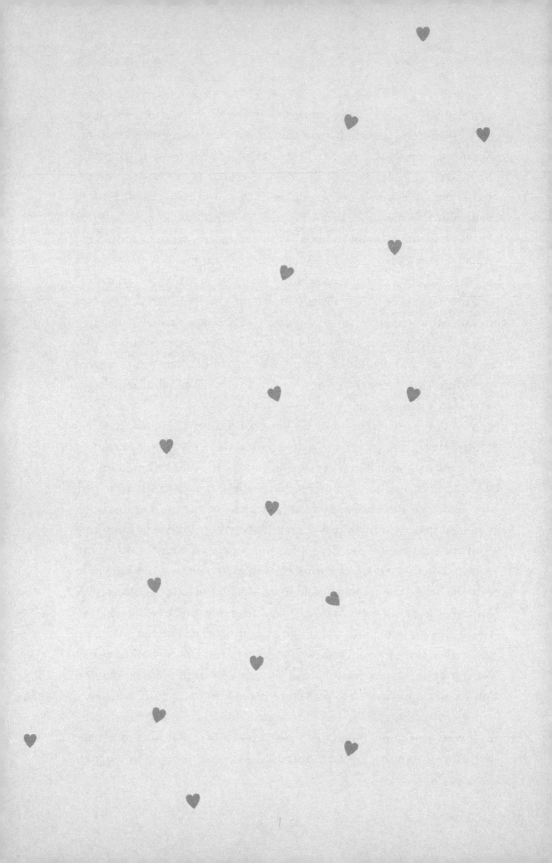

1

MYTH:
Your lover should
be your best friend

Okay, I know this is the mantra of every modern textbook and counselor, and I admit I've recommended it myself. But the goal of "best friendship" really isn't for everyone. Of course, the fantasy is almost irresistible. Men think of that best buddy they grew up with, who was their teammate, or who explored the neighborhood with them. Women think about their treasured schoolmate—and those times of sharing deepest secrets or the nights spent crying over dates gone wrong. We have a special place in our hearts for those pure moments with a best friend that few other relationships have equaled. We know a romantic partnership is different, yet many of us long to duplicate the intimacy and camaraderie of friendship in love and marriage.

But as sweet as friendship is, most people do not select a mate the same way they select a friend. We look for additional characteristics such as economic stability, erotic attraction, parenting potential, and so on.

Each of us has our own list of absolute necessities, but the truth is, when the whole list is put together, it is hard to find someone who has everything we need, and who is also our "soul mate." But, even if we are lucky enough to find that soul mate, there are good reasons to treat that relationship differently than a best friendship. I believe that if we try to make our love relationship a direct image of platonic friendship, we may defeat the success of a long-term relationship. A great friendship is a great gift, but we need to consider these problems:

Looking for a soul-mate friendship is bound to make most of us miserable because friendship just can't work in marriage the same way it does with platonic friends

Best friendship is often maintained by well-kept boundaries—one of which is sexual. And that is an important boundary because sex changes things. It creates jealousies, insecurities, desires—complicated emotions we don't have to feel with our platonic friendships. But sex is not the only boundary that differentiates love from friendship. Our best friends generally don't lose their tempers with us the way our spouses or lovers do: the passions aren't as hot, the hopes as high, the identification as close, the futures as linked. Our friend can stand back and be nonjudgmental or just hold our hand because his/her life isn't compromised or affected the way our partner's is. It's a safer relationship, and that's why so much love and support and steadfastness can be given.

And that's why it's damn near impossible to re-create that relationship in romantic relationships and why it's likely that sooner or later, partners seeking that kind of total support, exchange, and revelation (without negative consequences) will be disappointed. Is that fair? To ruin a perfectly good love affair or marriage because it isn't best friendship—to ruin something not for what it is, but for what it isn't?

This is especially unfair when we are talking about a marriage or co-habitation of over ten years. People change. And while you may have built up a good parenting partnership, trust, loyalty, and common interests, life may take you away from each other while you fulfill your duties of parent or worker. Many couples, maybe even most couples, find they are not as "close" as they used to be—but that doesn't mean they are unhappy with their family or each other. However, if they *think* they should be unhappy because they are no longer as intimate, they can make themselves unhappy. Is this really in any of our best interests? I don't think so.

It is particularly hard for women to get the type of best friendship that they idealize, and having this as a standard is rigging the relationship for disaster

Men and women have very different ideas of what being a best friend means. Be careful of these expectations. Most men grow up with a more modest definition of best friendship than women do. Friends are guys they do stuff with. There might be a few moments of talking about their deepest feelings, but the level of given, or expected, deepest feelings is pretty superficial and infrequent in terms of the way women define intimacy. On the other hand, women generally think that best friendship means sharing each other's deepest longings, mistakes, fears, desires, history—the more revealed, the better the friendship. They've learned this over years of having a best friend and intimate one-on-one times. A pioneering study by Janet Lever found that while boys are more likely to build friendships during team sports, girls do it over the exchange of secrets and feelings.

No wonder more men than women say that their wife is their best friend. Women have a higher standard—and most men haven't learned it. Women expect more conversation and more details and analysis about people. Men often take an overall estimation, aren't interested in as many details about people, and tend to be less active or adept at coding cues, analyzing feelings, noticing subtext. Women want their friend to be concerned about them all the time—and intuit when things aren't going well. Men don't seem to develop that kind of antennae. Women want a kind of intimacy most men simply haven't practiced—hence a great dependence on female friends as real best friends.

In fact, an unscientific marketing poll gave me some interesting data on this. About a decade or so ago, a market research firm asked couples with whom they'd like to be stuck on an island. Most husbands named their wives. But most wives named . . . Mel Gibson. Or, when they got serious, or more practical, their best girlfriend. While this little question was asked, and answered, in fun, there was an undeniably strong conclusion to be drawn that couldn't be ignored: Men have best friendships with women who do not think they are getting as good as they are giving. And a lot of them are mad because they think, theoretically, at least, that the guy they fell in love with should be more emotionally fulfilling than he is. He should be more capable of being a best friend.

Platonic best friends, by definition, don't have
to sustain sexual mystery and chemistry. So
what happens to a romance that has a
sibling quality to it?

When I studied one hundred couples who had egalitarian marriages, many of whom did report a very deep and close friendship together, it struck me that there was an unexpected casualty—and that was passion. Most of these couples were willing to accept this loss: The benefits they gained by creating a fair and equal marriage were huge. They had a partnership in parenting, economic contribution, and household maintenance. But this very closeness and intimate friendship created a relationship that took away one of the reasons for sex—and one of the ingredients of passionate sex: the desire to bridge the gap of intimacy between partners, the desire to reduce or extinguish distance and hierarchy. Sex, as a repairer of hurt feelings, or a renegotiator of power, more or less disappeared from these relationships. Couples could solve these issues through conversation and negotiation; they didn't need to use sex as their main (or only) way of reestablishing peace and trust. Without needing intercourse as the only theater for intimacy, sex became less necessary. In some relationships, sex more or less disappeared entirely. Some couples talked about having an almost sibling-like relationship—and even feeling a pale resemblance to the incest taboos that siblings might encounter. How can I have sex with a member of my family? Or more commonly, how can I have hot sex with my best friend? This loss of sexual responsiveness did not affect all peer couples—but it did affect quite a few, and is certainly something to consider.

Can most of us really withstand the insight and exposure that happens in an extremely intense friendship on a day-to-day basis?

There really can be such a thing as too much intimacy. One researcher calls it "fusion." Studies of lesbian couples, who tend to value friendship a great deal, show that they spend so much time together, become so similar, and have so much intimacy that sometimes one or both partners feels engulfed. The claustrophobic partner feels as though she has no separate identity—and she may leave the relationship because she feels she has to reclaim herself. While this is less likely in heterosexual relationships—there are simply too many differences between men and women for this kind of joint identity to occur—it could, and does, happen. There can be such a thing as too much intimacy; whether it is too much joint time or too much stripping away of private thoughts, some people feel they need to get away. Imagine really living with someone who knew everything, from whom you could conceal nothing, and with whom you were intertwined. Be honest with yourself. Would that really be comfortable? And be honest about something else: Have you *ever* really wanted intense intimacy— or has there always been some reason you wanted some distance and freedom? Just think about it. You don't have to buy the assumption of a partner who is a "best" friend if you don't want to. A standard friendship composed of trust, respect, collaboration, and mutual interests could well be not only good enough but also the best possible answer for you. Looking for a soul mate—baring all regularly—could be more exhausting than fulfilling.

These are not small issues—and they require a good deal of "out of the box" thinking and personal honesty in order to come up with a customized solution. All I am asking you to do is, before you try to duplicate your best friendships, look closely at yourself, your habits, and your prospects before you make any hard-and-fast rules about what your long-term relationship should be. There really are a lot of choices, and they don't have to be somebody else's. Some couples instinctively know, or learn from experience, that they work best together if they maintain some emotional privacy.

♥

For example, Karla, twenty-nine, and Paul, thirty-two, consider themselves partners and lovers, but they don't pal around with each other and don't try to be each other's closest confidant. They have both been in earlier marriages that self-destructed pretty quickly. Each felt their previous relationship was the victim of too much integration and too many expectations. Now, in their second marriage, they are very happy asking less of each other. Karla said, "I expected Al (her first husband) to understand me, my moods, my needs totally. He didn't, of course, and then I thought he was insensitive, unloving. Things got bad pretty quickly because I felt like he wasn't my soul mate. I also thought that the fact that he would take things to his buddies and not me was a real insult to our relationship. And when I would tell things to my girl-friends and not him, I felt that we weren't really meant for each other. We got more and more apart, and finally we both gave up on the mar-riage. Now that I look back on it, I think I asked too much from him—and I made both of us miserable."

Paul had been on the other side of that same problem. His first wife wanted so much from him that he felt claustrophobic. "She would not give me any privacy. She wanted to do all our activities together. I stopped playing golf with my friends and I missed that, but I thought when you were married you had to do everything together. But it was more than that. She always wanted to know what I was thinking. And when I wasn't thinking anything, she was hurt because she thought I was holding out on her. Finally, I *was* holding out on her. I started avoiding her. I really didn't want all that closeness, and I thought mar-riage had to include all of that. So then I thought I was destined to be single."

Both Paul and Karla had started with assumptions about marriage. Karla thought that a good marriage required knowing everything about each other, sharing everything, and always being on the same wave-length. When Karla and Al's talks didn't measure up to what she ex-pected from her same-sex friends, she felt the relationship had a terrible problem and her resentment (and his) affected how they felt about each other. Paul experienced it from the other side. He wanted some pri-vacy, some thoughts of his own, and he didn't want to feel as if their love affair depended on deep personal revelations all the time. Also he liked what he called "guy time."

By the time Karla's marriage broke up, she was tired of always being emotionally needy. While she was single she put together a very inde-pendent life, put her friends front and center, and worked hard to make a success of herself selling residential real estate. When she was fixed up with Paul by friends they had in common, she wasn't looking for the same kind of relationship she had had before. She liked his independence, his privacy, and she wanted her own. The fact that Paul had a real life of his own without her attracted her. She says, "I had learned to breathe on my own and I didn't want to give that up."

They dated casually at first, and she didn't take him too seriously. They were so different. He was a jock; she wasn't. He was an avid poker player; she liked to relax by reading or going to plays. But as she said, "We had a connection, and I listened to that. We were playful, physically wonderful together, and I respected our differences—in fact, they kept me interested. I felt together, but also free. I liked the space. I liked it a lot better than when I thought you had to be joined with your husband at the hip." Paul was pleased with the way things were going, too. "I'm a guy's guy kind of guy," he said. "I think it's okay to golf with Karla, but that doesn't replace my guys' weekends when we are betting on holes and we stay up late playing poker, smoking cigars, talking deals. I like that and I don't think it says anything about how I feel about Karla to want to do those kinds of things with the guys. She understands that. She gives me the time I need for myself. You know on the Meyers-Briggs test where it shows the kind of person who needs to be alone to collect his thoughts? I'm that person. She understands, and I appreciate that about her."

What both Karla and Paul learned was a way to have a lot of close friendships that supported their romance and reduced the pressure on them to be everything and do everything with each other. As Karla put it, "There are some things and ways that I feel that my friends are going to understand that Paul is either not going to appreciate or might even be disturbed by. I think it works better to keep those feelings elsewhere—and I don't begrudge that anymore."

For his part, Paul loves the freedom, the ability to be intimate some but not all of the time, and to have activities that he likes to do with his buddies that are not seen by his wife as a rejection of his marriage. Both Karla and Paul agree with her assessment of their relationship: "Of course we are close friends. But I would say that rather than Paul being my only best friend, he is one of my best friends. There are things he doesn't share with me, and vice versa. This may sound cold to some people, but I like the privacy, difference, and mystery."

So how do you have a happy marriage if you give up on best friendship?

As you can see, it's possible to consider your mate as your best friend, but there are a few things to keep in mind. First, know yourself. If you are the kind of person who needs a lot of personal privacy, who doesn't like to create a hermetically sealed primary relationship, who does need time to be with your friends and at your job, and who has no intention of exposing the nooks and crannies of your mind—make sure you are honest with yourself about that—don't pick someone whose vision of love is to permeate each other's soul.

Second, when you do fall in love, enjoy it—but don't be misled by it. You can enjoy that heady free fall into love and adoration and total revelation that occurs when a relationship starts; just don't expect it to last, or you will make yourself miserable and vulnerable. When we are newly in love, we have daily conversations that are intimate and revealing. We feel connected and we think we will never feel alone again. But this kind of intimacy is hard, perhaps impossible, for most couples to maintain. When it dissipates, as it usually does, it shouldn't be seen as a diminution of compatibility, sensitivity, or love. We deserve friendship, but actively being "best friends" may be expecting too much.

We can't help hoping that those first years of intimacy and friendship will stay fast and that our deep friendship with our partner will continue undiminished. In fact, more than that, we hope our friendship will not only stay undiminished, but will grow. But that's a little like hoping to strike gold in California. It can be done—there are many true stories about people who have done it. However, there are a lot more people who have to live with the fact that they have not discovered gold—and they never will. Should they feel bad about that their whole life? Should they keep prospecting because that's the only thing in life that makes life worthwhile? Or are there a lot of other ways to have a rich and happy existence?

Third, remember that you don't need a best friendship to have a great partnership. You can have fair play, a family you both enjoy, and a great lifestyle without being inside each other's head or experiencing the world together in the same terms. You can have good communication and fun together. All that seems ambitious, yet possible. Just don't expect the level of psychic unveiling that most female best friends expect—and you can be happy with what you have.

♥

I cannot tell you how many marriages I have known, interviews I have conducted, where one or both partners pour their heart out to me, bemoaning the fact that their partner is not their best friend. I often wonder: If they spent as much time with their best friend as they did with their partner, would their best friend still be their best friend?

2

MYTH:
You can't be in love with two people at the same time

L ove is supposed to be unique—almost by definition. In fact, one of the ways we know we are in love is that our emotional need and the intensity of our desire drives away thoughts of anyone else. If we are in love, true love, so the popular wisdom goes, we have eyes only for our beloved and—even more important—he/she has eyes only for us!

But wait a minute. We love our children; don't we? We love our mother, father? And then there's that first love, the love that got away but still holds a special place in our heart. When you think of it, the human heart really has a lot more capacity than we give it credit for. But maybe that's what we are afraid of—that we really *can* love more than one person, but we just don't *want* to. Few people want to share a lover with anyone else, even if they are personally capable of loving, and even taking care of, more than one partner.

But you may be unconvinced that it really is possible to have more than one true love; and you may think that those who have two people in their lives are kidding themselves about one or both relationships. I don't think so. I have interviewed many people who truly loved more than one person at the same time. Sometimes both relationships were sexual. Sometimes not. And I have experienced being in love with two people at once myself. Since I can't tell my own experience anonymously, let me give you some other people's stories.

♥

Betty is a woman who loves her husbands. Ah yes, that does sound strange, but in almost all respects she has had two husbands for twenty years. She married her first husband when she was twenty-five, and they have two children—a boy, currently in college, and a girl about to go. Betty and Allan had a romantic first ten years and then Allan, a less dynamic person than Betty, began to retreat from running their mutual business. He literally wanted to tend his garden and began a small business in landscape design while she kept the real estate office open and expanded it—in fact, franchised it. Their relationship, always warm and supportive, nonetheless became less totally engrossing, and Betty started spending more social time during the business day with her colleagues and clients.

One day she got a phone call for a special request—a home that was equipped for a handicapped person. She couldn't think of anything off-hand but made an appointment to meet with the client, to see what his needs were in order to think of a house that could be easily adapted. Her client turned out to be a single man, recently widowed, wheelchair-bound—and very handsome.

He also turned out to be very funny and Betty found that she liked spending time with him, looking at houses, trying to figure out which would be a good bet for modification. He was the victim of a terrible car accident (his wife was killed in the collision), and he evoked her sympathy and her admiration. Over time, they fell in love—but she did not fall out of love with her husband.

By the time I interviewed her, she had been with Wes for over ten years and with her husband for over twenty. She sees Wes as a family friend and as a lover. She is pretty sure that Allan knows that Wes is more than just a friend—but they have never talked about it. "I know that some people would think, do think, that this isn't fair to anyone—but I think it's fair to everyone. I have two men who love me, and I love them both. I am not fickle, really. It takes a bit of work, you know, to be a real partner to two people—especially two such different ones. It's not mainly about sex, although I think that's what a few of my friends must think. I think I was just meant to have these two people in my life. I think this was the path I was meant to take."

Is Betty kidding herself? No, I think there are different kinds of love, and each man draws a different version from her. Some people might say that she's really out of love with her husband and just found it inconvenient to leave. But if you talked to Betty, you'd know this isn't true. It may be that, being released from the passionate stage of her marriage, she can more easily take that energy elsewhere, but that doesn't mean that she no longer loves her husband, nor does it mean that her feelings for Wes are purely physical. She loves and takes care of both men.

♥

Here is another example. Norman has been married to Rose Ann since their last year of college. They are both fifty now. He is a high-powered litigator in a huge Chicago law firm. Most people think he eats nails for breakfast and can't imagine that there is a part of him available for sentiment, much less love. But Norman does make room in his life for two women, his wife—and a woman who is married to someone else. This situation has been going on for seven years.

"You know," Norman told me, "you can love people in different ways. I love Rose Ann as the mother of my children, as the center of our community, as someone who has been my only real friend most of my life. I would never desert her, and she has earned my loyalty. I have never been unfaithful except with Pia, and that was unexpected and it doesn't feel like an affair. It feels like another best friend, another person whom I truly and deeply love."

Pia is a set designer for the local equity theater but they met by accident, on an airplane. They were seated next to each other, chatted about their jobs, argued vociferously about politics, and the time passed quickly. At the end of the flight home, Norman, quite uncharacteristically, asked if he could call Pia sometime for lunch. Pia was unsure. She was in a "good enough" marriage and she knew that this lunch would have at least an undercurrent of sexual tension. But she was very attracted to Norman and told herself that she could just flirt and enjoy this a little without getting in trouble.

"It was all understood before the meal was over," Norman recalls. "It was such a powerful feeling between us. We couldn't keep our hands from touching. We were necking in the parking lot, which was incredibly reckless of me. I'm very well known in this town. It was a very selfish thing to do. I didn't want to hurt my wife. So I pulled myself away and said, This isn't going to happen."

But weeks later, he was calling Pia and said he wanted to see her. He did. And he was straight with her and she with him. He told her he loved his wife and he didn't know why he was acting the way he was with her, but it was a powerful feeling that he couldn't dismiss. She said she was in exactly the same situation, and they made a date to meet each other at a hotel in a week. That was more than seven years ago and they have seen each other about once a month, with a few exceptions, for all that time.

They both have qualms. Norman says, "I don't defend this. I don't justify it. It just is. I wish I could tell my wife. I wish I could tell my children. It saddens me that there is no word, no permission for this kind of situation. No one but Pia and myself can understand this, but I guess that has to be enough. I have two people in my life that are very dear to me."

Pia is even more troubled, but resolved to keep both relationships going. "I think you can love two people in different ways. I think of my husband as someone people would expect me to be with, artistic, a colleague, high-strung and neurotic as I am. We are two peas in a pod. But while we have a good life together and we love each other, we are not passionate together. Norman brings out a kind of passion in me I didn't know I had. So that is a different kind of love. I don't think I could live with Norman. He lives in a big house in Lake Forest and is very 'social,' plays golf, and is interested in a lot of stuff I couldn't care less about. But when I am with him I am more alive, more vibrant, than I ever am with Neil. I wish I could put the two of them into one person, but I can't. I know I am doing something wrong, but I can't imagine giving up either person. My life works because I have them both."

To some ears, this just sounds like the classic affair—a "selfish" man being unfair to everyone. Certainly people are being deceived, certainly neither woman is getting all of Norman's love and attention. Still, if we back away from the moral issues (for the moment, anyhow) I think it's fair to say that Norman is not being cynical. It is not a "purely physical" relationship with Pia, nor is it a "marriage of convenience" with his wife.

♥

There are other variations on this theme. For example, when an old lover surfaces from the past and while the present relationship is just fine, there is something special still alive from the old relationship. I have interviewed several men and women who "never got over" a past love even though they fell in love again. Not all these people had sex with their old flames, but in each case it was also true that the embers had never really totally cooled off. I interviewed a woman who quite innocently looked up her high school sweetheart when she found out he was in a city she was visiting. When she saw him, she felt an immediate tug at her heart. He looked very much as he had fifteen years before, and they both knew the old spark was still there. Both had been effortlessly faithful to their spouses up to that moment, and both knew that they were going to break that trust. They slept together that evening and they still see each other when they can. Neither of them wishes to leave what they feel are good marriages.

So can we really love more than one person? Absolutely. But should we? Even if we never have sex with the second person? Everything in our culture tells us not to. Whether we marry or not, most serious relationships are based on emotional monogamy, as well as physical monogamy, and any modification of that is considered faithless and immoral. Furthermore, even if we could get over the moral dimension (and few can or want to), everyone can tell you a story of a love affair that blew apart happy marriages and families. Maybe all that is true, but I think we should consider the following factors.

It is really hard to find everything we want in one person

There are probably good reasons to love person number one. He's great in bed, or she is the best mother in the world, or you make a great center of the universe together for family and friends. There is something special about each of you or you wouldn't be there in the first place (I hope).

But it is rare, rare, rare that someone is everything. Sometimes the very things that make him or her valuable ("He is the anchor that keeps me from being adrift") is also a deficit ("He has no sense of adventure—I can predict the future for the next twenty-five years").

When people fall in love with someone else, they don't usually fall in love with someone who is an exact double of the person they are with. They are usually interested in additional qualities that are missing in their partner. I know, the moralists out there (not to mention most therapists you go to) are saying, "Well, too bad. You selfish thing. So you don't have someone who is a tiger in bed. Big deal. Settle down, grow up, and don't betray anyone's trust." This is a fair admonition.

Usually the right thing to say. But it's a lot harder to do than it sounds. If you love someone but face a lifetime of missing an important thing he or she doesn't offer, it can be very hard to see that very quality in someone else, and turn away. In fact, many people break up their relationships because they insist that their lover provide everything they want even though no one person is capable of being everything.

Plus, it is really hard on relationships to ask that everything be provided to you. Sometimes you make your partner pay for that kind of demand. Long-term relationships go through many phases and discoveries. People change, and they might not retain their sense of adventure or they gain weight or they decide to become a professional polo player instead of a doctor. Even if big changes don't take place, things that were tolerated start to wear on the relationship. Many people supplement these losses with platonic friends, and that works for some things—but not if the missing element is sexual, romantic, or a desire to have a "soul mate."

There are three usual remedies for this situation "in house": grin and bear it; leave; or punish your partner for not being everything you want. Sadly, one of the most common responses is the last. How many times have you seen a committed couple tearing at each other for things that are not going to change. He is not a "go-getter," and she makes a cutting remark about that during a dinner party. Or she is not interested in his serious hobby, and he bitterly comments on how little they have in common.

But what if there is another person you love, who provides this sadly missed quality? Sometimes it makes the relationship seem whole, and there is less inclination to punish your partner for what he or she is (or isn't). Let's look at real life for what it is: If you are compensating for relationship deficits by having another person in your life, chances are your guilt over your behavior is going to make you act a whole lot nicer in your first relationship than you would otherwise (which is why wives are always a little worried when they get a gift and it's not Christmas, Valentine's Day, or a birthday). Your instinct is to do something nice for your unknowingly generous partner, unless you are really an unevolved sort of person who punishes your partner for the fact that you are in love with two people. (If you do, this might be evidence that this is not a situation you can handle and you should take one exit or the other.)

Loving two people makes you give each person some breathing space

Are you the neediest, most insecure person on the planet? Can you not bear being away from your lover? Are you so emotionally dependent that you scare away the people you want? The best resolution, of course, would be to figure out why you need so much reassurance and find a way to need less. However, failing that, here is a pragmatic suggestion: Allow yourself to love two people and then only ask half from each—thereby creating a whole and not swamping each relationship with your own neuroses.

I know this sounds a bit cold-blooded—but it might work for you if people tend to find a relationship with you claustrophobic. However, this solution works well only if you really are seriously engaged with both persons. If you are in love with one and just using the other, that's kind of ugly and selfish. No one should be made into just a place holder and, besides, it won't work. You will drop the second person like a hot potato if the one you really want shows up—and that will undermine the whole psychological balance of your endeavor. No, this has got to be the real thing: two people who make your life complete—separately as well as collectively.

It may be your nature

You may just be the kind of person who could *never* love just one person. Admit it. Stop making countless people who are more conventional than you miserable, and just be open and out there about who you are. Find two people who can share you—believe me they will be out there—or just find a couple of people (make sure they are the kind of persons who are not jealous, not inquisitive, and trusting) and be devoted to both of them. It may or may not work for you, but being with one person was never going to work out for you anyhow, and this might have a chance.

Life happens

None of the people I interviewed for my case studies had any intention of being in love with more than one person. Most had been very conservative all their lives and would have been very opposed, at least as far as they knew at the time, to anything but a committed monogamous relationship. But they met or reunited with someone special and for reasons specific to each one of them, they let these relationships grow and develop without ending their other commitment—or falling out of love with their previous partner. What allowed these dual relationships to exist? Maybe they were based on different kinds of love: one companionable while the other one was passionate. Or maybe the very thing that allowed the second relationship to exist and not destroy the first was that only one of these relationships was based in a supportable lifestyle while the other lover offered something that was best had in small or infrequent doses. What is interesting to ponder is that we have all been told that if you're really drawn deeply to another, it means the first love must be invalid. I just don't think that is always the case. But that doesn't mean that trying to love two doesn't have enormous risks.

The downside (Why not to love two people)

I would be breaking my vows

This is true, and it is one, if not the main, reason why many people would never allow themselves to love more than one person at a time. But remember this new infatuation need not be a sexual relationship—there are many ways to have an intimate and loving relationship (we have them with our friends) without becoming sexual. Perhaps sharing deep emotion, but not sex, would make this idea more understandable and less ignoble. If that is impossible for you, then think of it this way: Are you fulfilling the rest of what you have promised? Are you a good enough partner to be treasured and can you still expect to be a good partner in the future? If so, you probably fulfill your commitment in enough ways to feel good about yourself (and if you don't, you should worry about that). But of course, if your vows are sacred to you, the truth is you would not be "forsaking all others"—an important clause even if your second relationship did not become sexual. The guilt might never go away. Loving two people at one time might be something you cannot and should not do.

I don't feel good about lying, and I don't lie well

Well then, this really isn't for you! Because most open marriages where both spouses knew everything never work even when partners say they do. I'm not saying they're impossible to have. I actually do know several instances of them, more than I have put in this chapter. But the fact is that the ones that work are only a tiny percentage of the ones who try, and few people even try because they know that it would never even get past the talking phase. So for most people being openly in love with two people is going to be impossible, especially if they act on it sexually. Sometimes the most successful stories are those of people who have had a reconnection with someone or a small moment in their lives when they met another person they loved, but backed away from it pretty quickly because it was starting to corrode their marriage, main love affair, or personal mental health. Remember the book *The Bridges of Madison Country*? Why was it so wildly popular? Because everyone knew that a marriage could be worthwhile, but not exciting. The reader loved the idea that this housewife, tucked away in the anonymous Midwest, could have a deeply intimate and romantic interlude— and yet not sabotage her family obligations. The reader *wanted* the heroine to know passion and a deep connection of the soul with a truly worthy lover—and still not give up honor altogether by leaving. It was just the right mix: the right to have another love, another passion, but not another life.

Well, who said life was simple or easy? We are complex creatures. The myth we would like to believe is that we can only attach to one love in our life at a time. But that is not true. Our heart and our appetites are bigger than we say they are.

I might fall more in love with one person than the other and then leave my committed relationship

This is a serious thing to worry about. Because the truth is that when most people fall in love, they feel they have to choose. It is actually rare for people to manage loving two people in their life on a continual basis. (I think. But who knows how many people really have more relationships than it seems! This is not the kind of situation that people readily tell you about. You can't take a random sample survey and ask every third person if she or he is in a long-term relationship with more than one person.) Most people do seem to be into sequential monogamy. It is all they can handle to love one person. Two means they have to make a choice. This is the rule—and this issue is being brought up only for people who might be the exception.

3

MYTH:
You will know when you
have met "the one"

We've all heard the stories; in fact, my own mother had one. She was a secretary in a law office and my father, one of the young lawyers there, walked in and she took a look at him and said, "There's the man I'm going to marry"—and she did. There are other cases of people going out the first time or seeing each other and just *knowing*—or people going out for about three weeks, moving in together and living happily ever after.

But those are the stories we hear about, *because* they worked out. We don't hear the "I thought I knew" stories, where it seemed so right, and it wasn't. Of course, some hunches work out, and there are some cues that you respond to at a moment's notice. Most men and women have a sexual template that gives them those signals. As a lovely thirty-five-year-old classic Anglo-Saxon blond woman has told me, "If they are lefthanded bearded Jewish intellectuals, I am immediately interested!" For some people, it may not be a look, or even a kind of intelligence; it may be an "atttitude"—someone who has grace and charm with others—or perhaps someone who is cocky, a bit arrogant and sensual in the way he stands or walks. Whatever it is, the template encourages a "click" response, a feeling of instant sexual and emotional attraction. And if your template walks into the room, and you happen to be *his* or *her* sexual ideal, certainly sparks can fly and ignite. But just because this happens doesn't mean anything for the future, at least not so that you can rely on it. Knowing that this is "the one" is a myth for most of us for two reasons: There are so many false positives (she looked like "the one"—but she wasn't) and false negatives (he's not my type—and he turns out to be).

False positive

As soon as Sylvie walked in the room, Barry asked who she was. This wasn't unusual for Sylvie. A small, dark, extremely slim woman who had once been a professional ballet dancer, she still had the presence of someone who expected to be noticed and desired. Barry was taken with her almost immediately. As he remembered, "I called up my best friend, Sherri, the next morning and said, 'I know this sounds crazy, but I think I just met the woman I am going to marry.' I had this powerful attraction, unlike anything I think I had ever experienced before. I didn't have a name for it, but I thought, 'This is what people must mean when they say they fell in love at first sight.'"

Barry asked Sylvie out that evening and found her beautiful, vivacious, sophisticated, and stylish. He was proud to be with her; and he felt totally absorbed in her. "When she talked to me, I felt like there was no one else in the room. Actually, to tell you the truth, I felt there was no room."

Barry became increasingly convinced that Sylvie was "the one." Early on in the relationship, he gave her a piece of his grandmother's jewelry. He introduced her to his family and invited her on a family vacation retreat. He found himself thinking of her all the time, and he called her two or three times a day just to hear her voice. She seemed to reciprocate his feelings. He told all his closest friends that he had found his "true love."

When some doubts began to seep in, he tried not to listen to them. He was sure he was meant for this woman. They liked and disliked the same people, they both loved culture—the theater, good movies, and the symphony. They went to interesting parties together and he liked the business she had developed, which was putting together large charity auctions and parties. She moved into his apartment with him within six months of their first meeting.

Yet there were things about her that started to make him feel uncomfortable. He knew she had an extraordinary clothes collection but when he realized she went shopping more than anyone he had ever known, it surprised him a little. When he realized that she spent more money than she made on clothing splurges, it upset him a lot. They talked about it, and she put herself on a budget. But that didn't last.

He found that she was incredibly social. He liked being social, too, but she never liked being at home. He started to yearn for evenings at home watching TV and just making a sandwich. Many more things started to bother him, but when they would make love at night, or he would look at her just before they went out together, he was overcome with his desire to be with her.

But after two years of living together, the differences in some of their lifestyle choices and values became more than awkward; they became sources of contention. He felt they were spending way too much money. He was tired of her endless entertaining. And he felt that she didn't really love him the way he wanted to be loved. With some serious regrets, he broke it off. He said, "I just couldn't believe it wasn't going to work out. I read every fortune cookie as proof that we were meant to be together. I would even, I hate to admit this, read the astrology charts at the back of women's magazines to show why we belonged together. I guess if I hadn't been dedicated to this idea, we would have broken up a long time before we did."

False negative

The first time Maggie saw Rafe she thought he looked like a career-military type: not her favorite kind of guy. She was enamored of the GQ look, guys who knew an Armani from something bought at Men's Wearhouse and who looked like they had tackled the world and won. When her good friend Mitzi brought Rafe to a party as someone Maggie should meet, Maggie shot a "What *were* you thinking of?" look at her. However, when she talked to Rafe she really liked his dry wit and even though he still struck her as almost terminally midwestern, she agreed to have lunch with him in a couple of weeks.

She was incredibly busy ordering inventory for Christmas for her store, an exercise that always filled her with anxiety because guessing right on everything was as important as it was impossible. It was only at about a quarter to twelve that she realized she had this lunch date and it was across town. She jumped into a cab and into gridlock. She got there more than half an hour late, and he was just getting up to leave when she walked in. She apologized, sincerely, and he was gracious. But she worked harder at lunch than she would have because she felt guilty about being insensitive, and the two of them laughed a lot. She got a little more interested. Slowly, over some stops and starts, and some heavy working days, she started to see more of him.

It was the most lackadaisical dating she had done in a long time. There would be long times between calls and connections, and little early passion. However, one night, just when she thought this might be a nice platonic friendship, Rafe suggested a spur-of-the-moment trip to Las Vegas. She thought he was kidding. She had never been there, thought it must be the tackiest place in the world, and the invitation came out of nowhere. But she loved the spontaneity of the idea. So they got on a cheap flight and booked a room with two double beds.

One of the double beds never got used. They went out gambling as soon as they got there, and felt "like two kids in a science fiction movie." They ate and drank well and fell back into their room very sexually turned on to each other. The night was very passionate; Maggie wasn't sure where those feelings came from, but they were there. The relationship changed course at that moment, and about a year later they married. Maggie says, "I really never saw this coming. It took a long time to heat up, and I must have known him almost a year before we became lovers. If you had asked me if a serious relationship could start this way, I would have said no."

♥

Why do we hold on to this myth of "knowing" what love is? Well, because it's so reassuring, so romantic, it makes you feel that you have a fate and it just has to find you. We don't want to think that we passed up someone unique—that's too depressing—and we love the idea, indelibly impressed into our brains by countless movies and other media, that someone can walk through the door and we'll *know*. But this is the kind of fantasy that causes a lot of trouble. People act on it and people get discouraged and doubt their existing relationship. They rely on false or at least incomplete messages, and they make life-changing decisions based on them. Here's what could be turning your head and setting you up for a lot of grief.

You believe that this person is "the one," so you don't take in information that you should

Once you have decided that someone is the person you are destined to marry, you ignore information to the contrary because you don't want to know anything that doesn't support your belief. I have seen women watch their beloved scream at their children, or become highly agitated over nothing, or leer at high schoolers, and come up with a totally lame excuse for it. For example, Kendall started dating Loren and was so sure he was the one that, even though she hated it, she simply wouldn't take in the fact that Loren had three-martini lunches. She actually loved the way he loosened up when he was drinking and didn't want to match that behavior with the profile of other alcoholics that she knew. Even though she could see Loren turn into a different person when he drank, and even though she was aware that people who have total personality changes when they drink may be, or are, on their way to being addicted to alcohol, she chose to ignore what she saw and explain it away. Only after they were married and she realized that his drinking was undermining his work as well as their life together (he had ceased to be able to make love), did she look back and admit that she had had plenty of information about this. She just hadn't wanted to process it because she'd been so committed to her course of action. She had decided he was "the one" and after defining the relationship as her destiny, it took massive amounts of information and pain to change her mind.

You so believe this person is "the one," you lose your sense of self when the relationship starts to erode

Connie was not usually a superstitious person, but she had been told by both a fortune-teller and a Ouija board that the man she was with was the love of her life. She wanted to hear that. She was in publishing, he was her boss, she admired him, and she felt they were meant for each other. She knew, just knew deep in her soul, that he was "the one." When he started to make excuses, stay late at work, go off to book fairs without her, spend more time with one of the other editors, she was worried, but he denied anything was wrong. When she finally caught him and another editor with plane tickets for a weekend getaway, he admitted that he was having a second relationship and had just been too chicken to tell her. Connie went into a tailspin. She stayed home for the next week and wouldn't answer her phone or her e-mail. She sat in the dark and cried a lot. She wrote poem after angry poem—and then tore them up. She was distraught, and finally, when a couple of her good friends got really worried about her, she allowed them to take her to a counselor and the healing began. As she said, "I had my whole life planned. I knew that Tony was the man I had always wanted, he was the man I had dreamed about. When I lost him, I felt I had lost everything and honestly I wanted to die. I just bottomed out."

♥

If you feel someone is "the one," and the only one, it can be dangerous to your mental health. You assign someone else the power to make your life meaningful instead of assuming that if the relationship doesn't work out, another one will. Too much concentration on fate, on all the forces of earth bringing this relationship to fruition, make it more likely that you'll have an overdramatic reaction to the end of your dream. It's dangerous and it's not worth it.

You don't look at alternative explanations

Ever wonder why you meet "the one" at a certain time? Like when your biological clock is ticking, or after you have just suffered a big job loss (or a big job success), or, in essence, when events set you up and you are ready to have this perfect creature come into your life. There are a lot of influences that help you think that this is it, and they may have nothing to do with the person. Let me discuss two examples that have some interesting research behind them: (a) what you think your body is telling you, and (b) what you want and your need to follow the myths of your culture.

Your belief in the "truth of your body"

We often think that something special has happened when our heart starts thumping and our palms start sweating. These are supposed to be the signs of attraction and when they are intense, we think they are telling us that something really special is going on. But there is a lot of research to indicate that we may be misled into thinking that our body is telling us something important about a relationship when it is just notifying us of anxiety or danger. In either of these cases, adrenaline flows into our system, and the result is a full body alert. If we can define that moment as a romantic event, the full impact of these hormones make it much more likely that we are going to be seduced by our body into believing that we have had a "I just fell in love" moment. My favorite news clipping on this theme is one I cut out many years ago. It was about some famous NFL player who was telling how he met his wife. He was on a cross-country airplane flight and there was turbulence while the stewardess was serving him. Suddenly, the airplane had to dive many thousands of feet. Her tray went up in the air and she sprawled over him. The fall went on for several heart-thumping moments and, said the NFL player, "When we stabilized, I looked into her eyes and knew she was the one." Yeah, right. (I kept track of this marriage—it did not last.)

This gets compounded when you have someone rooting for a particular love interest. There was a famous experiment where they gave a lot of college guys pictures from *Playboy.* All these young men were shown centerfolds: one was a brunette, another a blonde, and the third a redhead. The men wore headphones as they looked at the pictures, and the headphones were connected to a device that would tell them their pulse and heart rates as they looked at each picture. At the end of the session, the guys were told that as a thank-you for their help in the experiment they could take one of the pictures home with them.

Most of the guys took the picture that had made their heart thump the fastest. The interesting aspect of this, however, is that the men were hearing false heartbeats, simulated heartbeats that were produced randomly by the experimenter and had nothing to do with how the guys were actually responding to the pictures. Still, because each guy *thought* his body was telling him something deep and true about his attraction to a given picture, he grabbed that one. Moral: We trust our body even more than our mind, and if we think we are excited about someone we give it a lot more credit than we should. If someone tells us, "You look like you are in love," it makes us think about it and take it seriously. Maybe they see something in us that reveals something really critical and true! And if we have a sudden surge of adrenaline, or we are in an intense period of our life, we may mistake that as a signal that because we are energized and intense while we are with our honey, that our general body response is telling us something important about our relationship.

You are addicted to romance

This is a romance-addicted culture. Did you see too many Disney movies when you were young? Too many Tom Hanks and Meg Ryan movies recently? There are so many wonderful films about people who were fated to be together—films that by skillfully blending music, suspense, gorgeous actors, and fabulous locations make us long, even pine, to be in the kind of relationship where you know you've met "the one." We are romance junkies and romance addiction is a nationally, even internationally, approved sickness. We celebrate love sickness: someone moping around, writing the name of her beloved on little pieces of paper, showing us bad poetry he has just dedicated to the person he is thinking about night and day. We enjoy seeing it and we want it for ourselves. The fact is that we also know, not so deep down, that this is, for ninety-nine percent of all people, just a phase and a phase that cannot go on forever. But instead of just accepting that, we want to believe that these feelings are the signal that we have found our soul mate. We want to believe that romance and passion tell us whom we ought to be with. Even when we find out, over time, that we can't trust these feelings, that they have misled us at least a few times, we still believe that these emotions will tell us about the significance of the relationship. What do I think? Enjoy the emotions, but don't rely on them.

You believe if someone was once "the one," she or he has to remain the one

Lillian Hellman once wrote, "People change—and forget to tell each other." Partners do change. And if they don't, you do. Someone may have been "the one" when you were twenty, but now at forty you are someone else. Maybe not entirely, but in many important ways, you are different. And the forty-year-old you has a different "one" in mind. Still, couples who long ago began to feel isolated or alienated from each other feel compelled to pretend that the relationship is still the same because they married when they were young and it's supposed to be for a lifetime.

I'm not saying this as an excuse to dump a long-term relationship. All I'm saying is that we live a long time and people often change their values and goals. If they do, there are really many people out there during a lifetime and the chances of there being only one that suits you (and vice versa) is slim to next to nothing. Overemphasis on the idea of a single person that is right for us, or the idea that some chemistry or magical insight will tell us right off that this is the person to stay with the rest of our life, is romantic, but it is not sensible. If you want to make a better choice do the following:

1. Respect your instincts, but don't rely on them. Give yourself time to know what is really going on between the two of you.

2. Tell yourself this mantra: There is more than one great person

for me in the world. I will not get desperate and do something precipitous because I believe it is this person or no one.

3. Remember: Just because he or she *was* "the one" doesn't mean you have to believe that forever. If things go sour, it might mean that it is time to go on to another one. You don't have to suffer forever because, at one time, this was true love.

4

MYTH:
Pick only someone you are madly in love with

As I have said, modern men and women are in love with love. We crave love songs, romantic books, and movies about starry-eyed lovers who triumph over adversity and end up together. We are envious when we hear stories about marriages that started with love at first sight. Most young people feel sorry for a couple who have a "companionate" marriage—a successful marriage based on friendship that never had a really passionate period. We love *love*.

The best sort of love is supposed to be "head over heels" love. We want "the earth to move" and even more than that, we are cautioned that if the earth *doesn't* move, the marriage is fatally flat. Our media reinforce this vision, over and over again. Let's take, for example, a movie that came out a couple of years ago. In *Meet Joe Black,* the female lead is told by her mega-successful, mega-smart father that he is worried that her reaction to her present suitor is too cool, that is, not over-the-top enough! He feels that she deserves to have a relationship that is like being "struck by lightning"—otherwise, she won't really have "lived."

The audience, if they haven't noticed it before, notes that the daughter isn't totally starry-eyed about her fiancé and agrees with the father (of course that might be influenced by the fact that they know the man she has yet to meet is Brad Pitt). We are first introduced to Pitt as he encounters New York City. He is sweet and, of course, gorgeous and intoxicated with the daughter at first sight, but so emotionally disoriented by their meeting that he walks straight into traffic and gets creamed. Seriously dead. No matter, his body is taken over by a spirit from another world, and, as fate would have it, the daughter gets to meet this handsome stranger again.

But even in this fantasy there is a warning. Brad Pitt isn't any ordinary Joe. His body has been taken over, for the time being, by none other than the Angel of Death on a sightseeing excursion. One might think he would be a hard nut to crack, but the magnate's daughter has captured his newly minted heart. He wants her; she wants him. Understandably Daddy isn't too keen on this match—he knows this is the Angel of Death, and even though his daughter is certainly feeling the kind of passion he told her validates a relationship, he doesn't want his child taken into the netherworld, away from the pleasures of ordinary mortals. Seems like a reasonable position.

But how does the audience feel? Well, kind of ambivalent. Oh, okay, so he is the Angel of Death—but so what? They *love each other!* Love is worth dying for. Love is the answer even if your husband has got kind of a bad job. Love is understandable even though he is going to take your father away from you. Love is a state of grace and justifies just about anything.

♥

The two worst myths concerning love are:

1. Love is enough to see you through

The Beatles told us that "All You Need Is Love," and we desperately want to believe them. But thirty-five years and an inflated divorce rate later, we know that love isn't always the answer; it may not even be half the answer. Love isn't a constant; it is highly dependent on life circumstances, our partner's emotional capacities and our own. If we are in love with love, then our relationships are inherently unstable because we are in love with a state of being that cannot be sustained. Love is a good beginning, but it is definitely never enough.

2. Life hasn't really been lived if you haven't loved with all your heart and soul

Boy, is this a hard standard to live up to. What does it really mean to love with all your heart and soul? What is it that is really the center of life? For some of us, it will be sacrificing creature comforts to make the world even a slightly better place; for others, it will be taking a difficult child and finding a way for that kid to have a successful life as an adult. There are many meaningful ways to live a life and while love is sweet, it is not the definition of a life well lived. Of course being infatuated is delicious, but the danger is that if we lift love too high we will sacrifice other great gifts of life in its service. Moreover, the description of love, in its tantalizing incarnations in the media, makes it hard for anyone to think they have had a love as good as the love they see on film. I think that by making romance so impossibly attractive many of us have experienced the feeling that we are missing out in life whereas, often, all we are missing is the Hollywood version of perfect love, as it exists in a moment of time, before the washing machine overflows, or hair starts to thin, or all the imperfections of real life come to bear. But we are hooked on the Hollywood vision, and this encourages us to marry that person while we are still infatuated. We want to have a time together before our romantic daze evaporates or mellows. Unfortunately, this means we make a commitment, drunk with our own emotions, before we know who it is we are really with.

So . . . I'm here to tell you that being madly in love isn't always the best way to enter a relationship—even if it isn't with the Angel of

Death—even if it's with a perfectly wonderful person. We have made too much of the need for obsessive love. We have put ourselves in jeopardy by extolling love madness, and I'll give you three good reasons why! Being *madly* in love usually means the following things:

You are literally producing poisons (called hormones) that make you act in ways that are not in your best interest

When you are madly in love (and I am not using this adverb by chance), your vision is clouded by total body discombobulation. Your groin is sending messages to your head that you are willing to have this person at any cost. Your brain says, Okay, I'm just going to ignore all these danger signals, these little pieces of information that are telling me this person is dishonest, or has an intermittent record of employment, or is morbidly possessive. In fact, I'm not only going to ignore annoying information that would get in the way of this wonderful feeling—but I'm also going to make a precipitate commitment just on the off chance that this wonderful being might stray to another suitor. I am, in other words, going to act like an idiot.

This of course leads to lots of bad outcomes, not the least of which is that you are ga-ga over someone who is devilishly attractive to you, but impossible to live with. Being madly in love tells you that the difference in your backgrounds doesn't matter, that his slavish devotion to his mother is something you can handle, or that her daily outbursts of temper aren't bad because she is so contrite and cuddly afterwards. Being madly in love might feel good up-front, but sooner or later, you will, unless you are really lucky, realize that it has led you to ignore some awesomely important facts about Mr./Ms. Not So Wonderful.

There are countless life stories that illustrate this point. Many people know, at the beginning of a relationship, some of the information that is going to make them gag at the end, but they just can't take it seriously when they are intoxicated. Derek, for example, knew when he first met Marsha that she was religious and he was not. He knew that she believed that life should center on the church community, and he knew that she tried to follow the Bible in her everyday life. He, on the other hand, was Jewish, agnostic at best, and the last thing he wanted to do was to hang around church-affiliated events. But he thought Marsha was the most beautiful, secure, loving woman he had ever met and, almost at first sight, he was infatuated with her. They started dating and enjoyed each other's company so much that he couldn't imagine life without her. When he asked her to marry him, she agreed, but put all kinds of conditions on the future: their kids had to be educated in church schools, their friends had to be people who respected her principles, they had to live near her parents, and he had to attend church with her on important holidays so that they could be a family together.

Derek says, "If you'd asked me before I met Marsha if I would have agreed to even one of those things, I would have told you you were crazy. But you can't imagine how much I wanted Marsha. I would have agreed to just about anything short of a sex change." So, Derek tried to be the husband Marsha wanted, even though most of what she wanted was extremely unfamiliar and uncomfortable for him. Still, in the early years, things worked, he fulfilled most of the bargain, and she gave him a little slack on some religious obligations. But as the years wore on and some of the infatuation wore off, each partner became increasingly less pleased with the situation. Derek felt cut off from his own friends. He was truculent about her church activities and went only reluctantly to visit her parents. When the issue of children came up, both of them knew that they could never agree on how to raise them, and each felt that made it wrong for them to have children together. When they knew that, they knew they had to end the marriage. Looking back, Derek says, "It just shows you how crazy you can be if you want somebody so much that the facts just don't matter."

You are picking a long-term partner on short-term emotions

Passion doesn't last forever. If it did, it might be worth picking a person just based on that alone—because while passion and intense love feelings are operating, the world is sure a yummy place to be. Alas, even the most passionate of lovers mellow out and, at some point, have to evaluate a marriage based on mundane, but critical, things like having or not having kids, creating a mutual parenting plan, living the lifestyle they expected, dealing with leaky roofs—those sorts of things. And those things can kill passion, if it isn't dead already. So being madly in love, while very, very nice, is just not going to last at the level people crave. Even if they are willing to live with a lout just because they are addicted to a hormonal high, the sad fact is that after about two years of cohabitation or marriage, the thrills start to go downhill. I suppose there are some relationships out there that stay as hot forever as they are for the first couple of years, but I would say if you are looking for one of those, you are looking for a needle in a haystack. Research, based on a national U.S. study, indicates that relationships stay hot for the first year and then sex becomes less frequent. Moreover, it is a rare relationship in which daily habits and crises don't have an impact on the emotional intensity of the relationship. Over time, what couples have left is the joint interests and values that make them want to remain married. They may be in love but not at the same fever pitch.

Pay attention to the principle of least interest—do you really want to be the person who loves most?

It is delicious to be in love, heady, thrilling. But guess what? It's not a very powerful position. Power is balanced when two people love each other equally. But, if you are the person who is loved more, you may feel a bit cooler than the person who loves most, because you are secure. You have the upper hand, at least just a little bit (perhaps quite a bit, depending on how intense your partner's feelings are compared with your own). If you love your partner but are not willing to do *anything* to keep him or her, you have the kind of emotional power that even a saint is likely to abuse. When you are loved more, you feel more secure, you get a few more favors, and you have a little more leeway in what you can say and do. When you are the person who is loved less, you are likely to be tap dancing your little heart out all through the relationship, always a little bit insecure (insecure in a major way) even if you are married with three kids. Only when partners love each other well, and equally, does reciprocity reign.

♥

Joan, for example, looks back at her love affair with Graham and realizes how totally he had her wrapped around his little finger. When they first met it was mutual and in fact he courted her, sent her presents, flowers, e-mail poems. Normally a bit cautious, she let herself be swept off her feet and then gave in totally. She started reciprocating the presents, writing him poems, leaving phone-sex messages on his answering machine so he would have something sexy waiting for him when he came home from work, and checking in with him several times a day by phone. Over time, however, she realized that he had stopped being the one who did all the emotional work and she was the one who called, wrote, and gave thoughtful presents. She found him cooler, more distant, and sometimes she couldn't reach him on the phone. He told her he wanted some "space," and that hurt her a lot. Finally, believing that he was no longer in love with her, she started accepting calls from Randy, a man who had been trying to catch her attention for a while. She wasn't too interested, but she knew she had to end her obsessive interest in Graham and also save a little self-respect. So she stopped giving Graham so much attention, and of course you know what happened. Graham started calling again, adding more heat to the relationship. Delighted, Joan dropped poor Randy and once again opened up to Graham. She let herself fall deeply in love again, and they moved in together.

But once they were living together, Graham started to be possessed again by his work and by his need for more privacy. Joan felt "on probation" and tried to be the best partner she could so that he would love her enough. She found that she was running his errands but he wasn't running hers, that she gave more massages than she got, and that she felt that he was always the person who said less reassuring things and made fewer promises for the future. "After two years of feeling like I was crawling on my belly and backing out of rooms so that I wouldn't disturb him I realized that as in love as I was, I just couldn't live this way. I just couldn't stand how much more in love with him I was than he was with me." She asked him for greater declarations of love, he couldn't or wouldn't give them, and so she left. Still, she grieved for that relationship for almost a year and felt very timid about giving her heart to anyone else for a long time.

♥

Do you *really* want to be *madly* in love? It is so painful to put your entire self on the line, to not be able to think about anything else in your life meaning anything compared to a relationship like this. This kind of love is the kind of love that makes you leave the job of the century, or not have kids when it was what you wanted to do your whole life, or suppress your own lifestyle for someone else's just because you would do anything to be with her or him. And the final result may be that you have given up too damn much.

So if being madly in love isn't the way to go, what's better?

Give the relationship time so that the madness passes and you are able to judge what you've got

It's okay to be madly in love for a while, but you need to be sane to pair up well. You need to see each other "in the clear light of day," and that might take a year or more. Relationships need to turn into friendships as well as love affairs before informed commitments can be made. It may be less euphoric to wait for more information before you set a wedding date or move across country and leave your jobs for each other, but it's a wiser path to take.

Carefully look at the balance of power between you and try to get a relationship that is fair for both of you

Make sure that love hasn't made you seem defenseless. Most people have a little bit of the bully in them, and your beloved needs to know that you will *not* do everything for love—you have boundaries, you have dignity, and you give yourself within those constraints. Your love will be more precious because it has conditions, not because you have handed over the keys to your soul. Partners who maintain individual strength have a mutual respect based on their ability to act independently and interdependently. Equality builds better habits, more negotiation than demands, more joint parenting, and more conversational equity (so that women get to talk as much men and there is active listening going on for both partners).

Contemplate a different model of love if it suits you

You know, not everyone is the hot-blooded, head-over-heels type. And if you aren't, you don't have to apologize to anybody. If you feel comfortable knowing someone as a friend, and getting to know and trust her or him gradually, if your sexual feelings and emotions develop gradually, there's nothing wrong with you. In fact, you have an advantage. You can take in more information with better common sense about it than people who meet and commit operating from the "I have to be hit by a thunderbolt" theory. Your kind of love isn't inferior. And it's probably a lot safer.

But one caution ...

It's best not to have to be madly in love. But be careful, and as Shakespeare said a long time ago, "To thine own self be true." Some people do get tired of the ups and downs of romance and decide to "settle"; that is, they really want to marry a trapeze artist, but, a few drastic failed love affairs later, they are ready for a less exotic creature. That's fine if you've really changed and want a calmer, friendlier, less exhausting lover. But if you are just "making do," as opposed to really changing what you want, your change of heart is unlikely to stay satisfying and you are unlikely to be able to sustain the new kind of relationship. You don't want to be so much less in love that you are not in love at all and turn into one of those meanies who cause their partner pain and suffering. If you are a love junkie, and there is nothing you can do about it, so be it. But know that it puts you at real risk. And try to give the relationship time so that when your hormone potion eases off, you haven't made any commitments you can't cancel.

5

When you want to get serious, date only people with marriage potential

So, you are twenty-eight and you think it is high time you should get married. Or you are forty-five, divorced, and afraid that there will never be another love in your life. You have no patience for going out with frivolous people who are not into commitment, or portly middle-aged types whose idea of settling down is to let gravity take its course. You only want to go out with someone who is a likely nominee for love of your life. Time is against you, and this is logically the right thing to do—yes? You can't believe I am going to take issue with this one, can you?

Well, I am because, basically, I don't care what people say. They are much more likely to get *older* than *wiser* about love. In fact, in some ways I think people get less able to date well because the older they get the more they declare they are "set in their ways" and they know what they like and don't like. But people don't always get what they think they want. For example, let's take people who ask you to fix them up.

You pick out who you think is the perfect match for them and they are insulted. They come home with the person they are thrilled with and you are aghast, or at least surprised. They said they were only interested in tall, thin, dark women and what they've chosen is a short, plump redhead. They said they wanted a creative, artistic guy. The love of their life is a quality assurance specialist in a bean factory. Go figure.

So it's not always clear what someone wants because there are a lot of surprise packages out there that turn the rules upside down. And if you are only going out looking for marriage prospects, you may miss a whole category of quality merchandise that you are simply too ignorant to be aware of or too scared to try. Let me give you an example from a friend of mine.

My friend Lee had put together a thriving local business. She was a part of the "in" social crowd (even though that wasn't her background), and she was a force to be reckoned with in the financial world. Lee had many good friends and a wonderful place to live that she had built herself. But she was forty years old and had been married only for a short time in her twenties. She was lonely and she wanted to get married. She would think to herself, "I have beat the odds putting together an amazing business from nothing. If I am smart enough to do that, why aren't I smart enough to find someone who I can love and marry?" Lee is nothing if not brave, and she decided to put the same kind of fastidious research into this question that she would if she were figuring out a new business endeavor. In her search, she came across a course that someone was teaching called "How to Get Married." Now, a prouder or more timid, or self-conscious, woman would have laughed and turned the page. But not Lee. She called up, liked how it sounded, and signed up.

I won't go into the whole course here, but the instructor had two requirements that I thought were brilliant. First, you had to meet ten new people a week, even if that required standing by an elevator and shaking hands; and second, if anyone was friendly and asked you out, you had to say yes—even if the plan was for only twenty minutes in a well-lighted room and you had your buddies positioned at a nearby table to rescue you at the wave of a hand!

Lee dutifully started meeting people, but the one who mattered most came to her. He came to her firm to meet with someone else, met her in passing, and because he is a friendly, sweet guy, chatted her up just for the fun of it. He had such a good time of it that he asked her if she would like a cup of coffee. The old Lee would have said no. This man was fifteen years younger than she. He was good-looking, but he looked like a kid to her. And she noted that he had a shriveled right arm, the consequence of a birth defect. Lee, a serious sports enthusiast who had built many of her relationships around tennis and golf, would have considered this a deal breaker in the old days. But the course said to go out with anyone, so she, being the good student, accepted the coffee date.

She found Anthony totally enjoyable. He had great enthusiasms, he was involved in a number of different projects as a city land-use planner, and he was clearly taken with her. He asked her out for dinner. She accepted. The rest, as they say, is history. They dated for a year, had a big, fabulous wedding, and are happily married, twelve years later. "But," you protest, "this was an accident!" You think it could never happen to you and you offer the following counterarguments:

I know what I like—I don't need to waste time

And I say, review whom you have dated—or, for that matter, married. If you were so wise about everything, why aren't you happily married or cohabiting now? Nobody, and I mean nobody, I've ever met has had an absolutely perfect record. And think about all those people you dismissed in high school as nerds, or jocks, or whatever category you loathed and consigned to the trash heap. Aren't there a few of these people whom you were wrong about? People who went on to be fascinating or who achieved greatness in some way that makes you look at them differently now? Admit it, haven't you made a few mistakes?

Here's my answer: You *do* need to "waste" time. You do need to assume that you don't always know what you like and who is worth knowing.

But I'm expressive: if I don't like someone, he or she will know it

And you want me to support that statement? Get over it. This is a good time to learn how to delay judgment and see what there is about even an obnoxious person (or an awkward one) that gives you new insights. For example, Ruth told me about her first date with Ethan, a painfully shy man who normally would have sent her scurrying to the bathroom for an escape route. But because Ethan was her brother's best friend at college, she felt compelled to be extra nice to him, and when he invited her to his studio to see his artwork she politely accepted. What she saw there dazzled and moved her. Suddenly she thought of him as a genius with a deep and intricate soul. And when he talked about his and other people's art, a new Ethan emerged, a careful but passionate thinker who intrigued her. She would never have known that if she had given in to her usual abrupt "I'm out of here" style.

I have certain requirements, and if I know this person can't possibly meet them, I'm just not interested. I've dated enough, I know enough

Personally, I think you are just jaded and boring. You can never know enough. People are full of insights, or maybe just their lives have messages in them for you even if you never want to see them again. Somebody smarter than I said a very true thing once: that everyone's life is worth hearing—but that only truly interesting people have more than one story in them. I think that is true; everyone's life has a message in it—and you can learn something about yourself and life in it. What you have to do is *learn how to be a good interviewer rather than a passive receiver.* Of course you are bored if you let someone rattle on and you find yourself listening to details of why natural fabrics are "out" this year. But if you picture yourself as an interviewer, someone who can use this moment to find out what this person's life has been like, their experiences, failures, successes, hopes, or even just their opinions on things you've been thinking about, I guarantee you that you will have something interesting to take home. A word of caution, though: If you are a good-enough interviewer, four out of five of these people who have never been taken seriously in their lives will fall in love with you, follow you home, and live on your doorstep.

There really are good reasons to see people who you imagine, maybe quite rightly, could never be important in your life. Some of these reasons are practical, and some of them pertain to the theme of this chapter—that you never know what lurks within a person unless you give yourself enough time to find out.

Here are the reasons to rethink your position on this that I think are important:

We need time to get over our first lack of attraction

Most of us are visual creatures. But we usually are attracted to someone, or not, on a ten-second look. Some people need to be viewed a little longer to see the beautiful parts of them. Some people do become more beautiful as you know them better. This takes a little time, so if you make quick judgments you may never give this transformation a chance to happen. Also, people have hidden talents and interests, or they may be in transition themselves. If you decide they are not marriage material before you know any of this information, you may miss a great bet. What would you have thought about Bill Gates if you had just seen him around the water cooler? You probably would have miscatalogued him. Believe me, even if he hadn't become supernova wealthy, he was husband material before, and if he were single you would certainly consider him now!

You are still a work-in-progress

When you decide someone isn't "marriage material" before you have given yourself a chance to get to know her or him, you are also making the assumption that your life has a certain invariable script that must be enacted. How tedious! How likely to sell life shorter than it has to be. You might want to think of life as an adventure and this person as an illustration of one of its possible trips. Sure, he or she may be exactly what you don't want—but then that crystallizes what you don't want again—you've checked in and reaffirmed that's not where you are at. Still, you might find that if you are really listening and thinking, this nutty, high-spirited person is *exactly* what you need to shake up your life, even if it isn't taking you to the altar (but then again, who knows? If you get to know him or her a little better, he or she might have a serious, well-grounded side). Don't say you couldn't be happy with someone who likes to meditate. Try it for a while and see if this actually brings something new and useful to your life. Are you a big-city guy who just met a farm girl? Don't close the door before you've taken time to breathe in the fresh air. In any case, you get my general point: Don't assume you are the same person you were last week. Give yourself a little room to grow and let meeting these other people help you do that. Broaden your horizons. You may have sold yourself an image of life and of yourself that can, and maybe should, be modified.

Maybe one of these people can teach you something sexually new

Okay, so you want a nice, grounded person whom you will live with in a big house in a safe neighborhood and take vacations to the same places your parents did. Okay. I accept that. But in the meantime, some of these people you are meeting may teach you something that isn't in *Better Homes and Gardens.* Sometimes the best lovers are the best lovers because they are strictly non–marriage material. Let me tell you about the cowboy I once . . . No, we will skip that in this chapter, but you get the idea. This is your time to explore parts of your body and your psyche that will be something you can perfect and offer to the person whom you eventually fall in love with. You can use this time to forget about faking orgasms, or pretending you know everything, and become a good student. That passionate player who would be a terror as a marriage partner is just the person to teach you those things you missed in your sexless first marriage. Sometimes it's good to be the teacher—especially at the Ph.D. level—and sometimes it's good to be a student. Knowing you are not playing for keeps gives you the license to be honest and maybe a little bit over the top. (When was the last time you needed a soundproof room?)

♥

Hal, for example, married his childhood sweetheart and never had sex with anyone but her. When she left him at thirty-nine, he not only felt emotionally awkward going back on the dating market, he also was terrified about how he would do in bed. During the last year, his wife had made him feel totally sexually inadequate. He worried that she was right, and he felt terrible about himself. He found that during his first forays out on the dating scene he shied away from more than necking with someone. He was maximally respectful, and part of that was that he didn't want things to go further. He was sure he would be incompetent.

People kept fixing him up, though. He was such a sweet guy, everyone thought of him for their other sweet friends, and this resulted in a lot of sweet dates that never became passionate. One day, however, Hal was in a bar relaxing with some guys after work when some women waved them over to their table. They all went, laughed, and drank until Hal was feeling no pain—and feeling a good deal of sexual interest in one of the women. She was about ten years older than him, attractive, and sexually aggressive. She kept her leg next to his during the time everyone was there and then, somewhere along the line, he felt her hand very, very near his crotch. This had the desired effect and, when she whispered into his ear and invited him over, his besotted brain didn't have time to say no.

Once he got to her place, however, his fears kicked in and he told the woman how inexperienced and nervous he was. She seemed to like the challenge and while that first evening wasn't Olympic-class lovemaking, it was fun and Hal loved it. He continued to see her for months, and they became friends rather than falling passionately in love. He learned a lot from her and they had good times together. Neither of them thought this was a relationship for the future, but both knew that it was exactly what they needed for the present. For Hal, it was his transition to being able to be confident enough to meet someone who could be a long-term commitment.

Maybe one of these people can teach you something emotionally

Lois was a good Jewish girl who only wanted to marry a Jewish boy. But she found herself working overseas where there wasn't another Jewish person for hundreds of miles. She started dating non-Jewish guys and found a big surprise—because she "wasn't serious" she was being more straightforward, less coquettish, and more honest. She found she liked her new persona, and she began to realize that she had sold herself short before—and come up shallow. When she moved back to the States and started dating men who shared the cultural and religious background she prized, she still kept her new self with her. She had learned more about herself and was grateful for having had the chance to date without being "on the hunt."

Dating noncontenders will help you lighten up—so that when you do meet the right person, you won't suffocate the person

There are few things so unattractive as someone desperate to get married. Have you ever dated someone who is dying to get married or settle down? I don't care if you are gay, straight, or undecided—this experience is a big turnoff. This might be a terrific person, someone you might be interested in, someone you *were* interested in until it became apparent that this person was so needy and so determined that it mattered less who you were and more how quickly the deal could be closed.

Worse, and be honest now, is *being* that person, watching yourself overwhelm and scare someone off because your emotional needs were too near to the surface. Finally, you had found someone who really interested you and you started inviting him or her to Paris with you that weekend or casually commenting too early on what great children you could produce together. Before the entrée came you knew you had been too much, too soon. But it was impossible to start over.

There is a cure for this. The cure is to keep yourself busy, amused, and interested in a number of people. The cure is to be happy, be learning, and to treat each new person as a possible addition to that stable of teachers as opposed to a soul mate and savior. With any luck, someone special, who becomes uniquely dear to you and, ultimately, a lifetime partner, will emerge from the pack. But only if you give it the space to happen. So, in the meantime, it is good planning to outsmart your needy little heart. Get to know a lot of people, even if there is no neon sign overhead saying "Marry This One!"

There are a lot of people who will be well worth knowing and have something to teach you. If you are a volatile person and date someone who hates drama, you learn to control yourself. If you are heading toward an ambitious career, but start seeing someone who sees that as an impediment to a meaningful life, you might learn about spiritual or philanthropic parts of your personality. You are not "wasting time," even if these people are so different from you that a real match is an impossibility. They expose you to new potential choices and draw things out of you that help you grow. They may not make you totally different, but they develop your range of emotional skills and self-knowledge.

6

MYTH:
You should be similar to your partner

Okay, I grant you, this one has something to it. It's important to be comfortable with someone. You don't have to look over to know your partner is thinking the same thing you are thinking. You see life in the same way so often, it makes you feel that you were meant to be together. You see people the same way; you are not hard on each other's friends. You don't have to work hard to understand each other. The relationship effortlessly feels like a good fit. You understand each other's background. You know how you got to be the way you are. All in all, you both are incredibly at ease. You share important values, and life goes by unquestioned. Whoa there! I knew there was a reason I picked this one: because this is the first fly in the ointment—similarity can breed not only comfort but boredom and, most heinous at the turn of the millennium, zero personal growth. If you are with someone who is absolutely like you (which, fortunately, is rarely the case), similarity brings good news and bad news. The good news is that, like other kinds of twins, you are a force to be reckoned with. You power along, firm in the mutual sureness you give each other that all may be crazy elsewhere but your little island of togetherness is just right. Your passions are similar, you work well together, like and dislike people together, and have the same tastes. You are close—but you are a closed system. Yet I don't think that's the worst thing about too much similarity. The worst thing is that some people are scared of any sort of difference. Let's talk about some common reasons that people avoid one another that I think are often seriously wrongheaded.

Differences in ethnicity and race

We human beings are a tribal lot, and the majority of us seek out our own kind. I understand that religious similarity (and consequently agreement on how to educate children) and knowing a great deal about each other as soon as you meet are important values to consider. Still, I think our clannishness is a shame. I have watched all kinds of "mixed" marriages in my own extended family (Caucasian, Chinese, Hispanic, African American), and I can say, without a doubt, that when we all get together, the parties are a lot more interesting.

More than that, there is an excitement, an energy that comes from simply putting different ingredients together and letting them find their own way to be flavorful. Whatever the combination—Eastern European Jews with Norwegians, or Brazilians with East Indians—the new mix gives each person a new tradition, a new family history, and an additional number of loyalties and customs.

Now I know many people have been fed, right along with their mother's milk, the idea of keeping their ethnicity constant and their race pure (fat chance of that for most of us). If this is critical to you, then by all means don't test yourself—you'll probably make yourself, and what's worse, your partner, miserable. The divorce statistics are higher for people of mixed race, religion, and maybe ethnicity (a lot harder to measure). But I think that's the holdover from a different era. I think ethnicity and race, central as they are, are not the essential similarities that truly matter. In fact, in an illuminating study by sociologist Martin Whyte, reported in his *Mating, Dating, and Marriage,* a random sampling of people in the greater Detroit area showed that ethnicity did not predict breakups at all. Stability was more related to early levels of love and commitment.

Differences in age

In general, our culture promotes marriage between people of similar ages. When an older man marries a much younger woman, we cluck—it seems to us a privilege of age and money rather than a love match. If an older woman marries a much younger man, we scoff, predicting that he will leave her eventually for a younger woman once he gets over his "mother complex." The couple themselves know they are seen as ridiculous by others—and most people think of it, at least at first, as a transitional relationship even if the couple really is totally attracted to and compatible with someone much older or younger than themselves. Parents look at a twenty-year difference between their child and a suitor and want to call the police rather than the preacher.

But while there are good reasons for caution, there are also some reasons to rethink our feelings about this. True, differences in age can mean that the older and younger partner will have different energy levels, incompatible friends, out-of-sync timing, and impatience with some of each other's concerns. Still, every relationship is a mixture of costs and benefits, and the only important thing is to know what you are trading for what. Older women living in long-term relationships with a lover or spouse surely wouldn't want someone who was exceptionally keyed in on youthful good looks. Appearance changes over time, and people are insecure about their looks in the best of circumstances—much less with an attractive younger partner who is looking for the same. But assuming the relationship was built on a number of important characteristics (accomplishment, charisma, flair for living, intelligence, whatever), the relationship need not be some kind of Oedipal mistake.

♥

Vicki, for example, was a patrician woman of considerable wealth. Her family had come over on the *Mayflower,* and her interests and activities were predictable with her class origins: hiking in Tibet, "good causes," and intense gardening. People lifted more than a few eyebrows when, at age fifty-two, long divorced from her first husband, she began dating Kent, a thirty-four-year-old associate professor at Boston University. Kent was a charming, intelligent man but hardly to the manner born. When the two decided to live together, her friends and family thought Vicki was being taken for a ride. Although everyone liked Kent, and thought Vicki was a plenty savvy woman, the general opinion was that he was marrying her for her money and status.

"Well," says Kent, in his mid-fifties and still with Vicki, now seventy-two, "I suppose there was some of that. I come from a working-class Detroit family. Why wouldn't I be attracted to the class and comfort that Vicki offered? But, I had already achieved so much. I didn't need her money. I just adored everything she was. People underestimated me. They thought I couldn't appreciate the other things about her to love her. I loved her intelligence, her enthusiasms, her purity of spirit, her way with me, I loved *her.*"

The marriage has had its ups and downs—Kent did have a flare-up of an old affair—a person he had known before Vicki. During that time he was more distant from Vicki, and she was worried—but never asked Kent what was going on. "Vicki is a true gentlewoman," says Kent. "I know she thought I was having an affair. But she would never ask. We had made an agreement there were things we would never want to know but that we hoped they would never intrude in our relationship. I feel bad that I let that affair affect us, but it's over now and we're okay again."

If you ask Vicki how she would rate her marriage, she says, in her upbeat and forthright way, "An unqualified miracle." That doesn't mean she pretends that it has been without heartache, but rather she believes that, regardless of low points, that they really were the right match for each other.

♥

There are also good reasons for older men and younger women to combine. The common case we hear about, of course, is the marriage for beauty and validation. The vision of a trophy wife is the most common and the least reassuring example because the choice has been almost entirely based on youth. But that tarnishes all relationships between older men and younger partners (including same-sex partners), and there really are some lovely and useful things that can happen because of an age gap. Some younger women really don't want be with a man during his twenties or thirties when he is most likely to be absorbed in his work and less interested, or able, to compromise. Hard-driving, ambitious men don't mellow enough to be true partners until relatively late in life and many women are willing to take the deficits that come with age, for the generosity, kindness, and insight that might also be present. And of course there is the "great man" syndrome, where younger women are thrilled to be in the world of someone of great accomplishment or wealth.

Frannie, for example, was, like most of her fellow music students, totally mesmerized by the conductor who came in a few times a week to teach graduate students. She thought he was distinguished, handsome, a handful, and utterly fascinating. She was radiant when he complimented her on her playing. The fact that she was twenty-one and he was thirty-six did not faze her in the slightest. She dreamed about him and counted the hours until the next class would come around. She found every excuse she could to be alone with him.

She wasn't quite sure when it happened, but at some point she noticed that he was staying longer after class and it seemed to her that he was looking for reasons to be in her company. He was friends with her parents, who were well-established musicians, and he seemed to be finding more reasons to come over. Finally, he asked them, in an old-world sort of way, if he could have permission to see their daughter. Frannie was thrilled, her parents much less so. But Morris was clearly a musician on the rise, and his musicality was ultimately more important to them than his age!

It was an intense love affair and they married, though Frannie's friends were worried about the age difference and the fact that it became very clear that her career would come far second to his. But the truth for Frannie is that she wanted to be relieved from the burden of being a concert performer. She was more than happy to tuck her career away and concentrate on having children and protecting Morris's flank from the politics of the concert world. Twenty years later, even though she would admit to many drawbacks (such as most of their friends being his age or much older), she says that her choice had been just right for her.

♥

What are the risks? Well, the older person could die sooner or need a tremendous amount of care that would age the younger partner before his or her time. The younger person could dash off just at the time when the older person was most vulnerable. The younger partner might miss having a spouse who is young and vigorous, or the older partner, ready for retirement or slowing down, might find the more hectic lifestyle of the younger mate inconvenient or a bad fit. These things are true enough. And yet, there might be years of a really great relationship—and no one is ever guaranteed what will happen in any relationship. Being the same age carries no guarantees. Half of all first marriages in the United States end in divorce—and most of these marriages are between people who have only a couple of years difference between them. What is important is that the age be less of a cost than the sum of the relationship's benefits. Age difference can be a benefit for a long time. For some people, the specific person they fall in love with is worth any adjustments the age gap may require.

Differences in politics

One of the criteria people use to decide the suitability of a potential partner is that the person agree with all their political positions, and I mean all of them—from presidential elections to policy issues such as health-care reform.

While agreeing on these things does give a couple a sense of common cause, I just wonder if it should be quite the sorting mechanism it is. It is rather boring to agree on all your political positions because then you never have to defend any of them, look for real data to support your positions, or really examine why, and if, you feel strongly about them.

In theory, we know that differences add to the spice of life. The old Katharine Hepburn–Spencer Tracy movies were hung on the idea of differences and sparks being ignited from attracted combatants. Certainly, the modern-day marriage of Mary Matlin and James Carville, professional political operatives from opposite ends of the political planet, indicates that sometimes strong opposing political views don't prevent people from having enough in common in other realms. In fact, some people, and you might be one of them, enjoy the discussion and the challenge as much as they care about the answer—as long as they are treated with respect. In the case of Matlin and Carville, they both enjoy politics so much that it seems more important that they live in the same world of intrigue and competition than that they support the same candidate, or even social policy! Is it really important if your mate is of one party affiliation or the other? Always liberal or conservative? Maybe not.

Differences in size

I have always found it strange how much some women care if a guy is taller than she. Not that I have any authority here: Any guy who is shorter than I is a member of the circus. I am so small I cannot help finding men taller than I—and I did. But I think I missed out on meeting some wonderful small men because I was afraid that if I got paired with them, we would look diminutive together—and I wasn't ready to look any smaller than I was already. But I had my values all wrong. It is interesting to me that as I got surer of myself, I found more short men attractive—and even though I didn't end up with one, I could have.

This is a really important lesson for tall women to learn. It is a stupid distinction to make when height standards cut out more than 50 percent of the men they might be interested in. Likewise, I find it odd when men have strong preferences for tall or for short women—I get the fact that we all have individual templates for sexual attraction. But you know, you can grow out of some of these—and not miss someone special.

Differences in interests

There are some interests that might truly be important to be well matched on. If you are a person whose whole world becomes meaningful only when you are kayaking, climbing a mountain, or running a marathon, it might be hard for you to be with someone whose idea of a perfect Sunday is doing the *New York Times* crossword puzzle. Still, most of us have a wide range of interests that we can pair up with other people, and we are capable of inventing new ones. I think it is less important that you share specific interests with someone than that you both have the same level of finding things interesting. For example, some people take enormous joy in the discoveries of everyday life—from a great new cheap place to eat to an article in the paper about digital technology. It might not be important that their spouse is interested in all the same things they are, but a general ability to be intrigued and interested would be critical. Likewise, a person who is happy preserving the same friends and interests she or he had in high school or college may be ill suited to a partner who always wants to explore new hobbies, places, and people.

This brings up a few other things I *do* think are important to have in common.

Energy/intensity levels

Over time, I think there is nothing more important than who wants to sit and who wants to stand up, who wants to explore and who wants to let be. If people aren't matched on this characteristic, one person feels pushed and dragged and the other person feels held back and extinguished. These are terrible feelings because for one person peace and pace are being ruined and, for the other, the whole world is being lost. It almost doesn't matter whether the issue is having friends over, travel, or going to see a movie. If I were sorting out the world, I would make this the first cut.

Empathy levels

Some people wouldn't notice if you burned all their clothes—others notice if you bought a new cologne. It is not uncommon for one partner to be depressed for a significant period of time while his or her spouse is oblivious that this has gone past simple moodiness or sadness. This is bad enough, but it is very hard if one person is sensitive to all the cues of the other person and the other is completely oblivious. Not everyone has a keen interest in noticing or interpreting their own actions, much less their spouse's (though many wives have resolutely kept hoping that their husbands would eventually develop intuition and empathy), and I say if it doesn't look like it's there—it's not. Of course, women can do what women have always done—invest in their girlfriends and get nurtured from them. But today's men are better, and there is no need not to get paired on this one.

Plus, it's not always the man who is cold and closed off. For example, one of the incidents contributing to Dick's divorce was his wife's absolute inability to empathize with what he was going through when his business was being sued. Everything was at stake, he was a named a defendant, and she simply never showed up at the trial. Even people who didn't know them very well asked if something was wrong with the marriage. Dick was so humiliated that he made excuses about why she wanted to be there but just couldn't. When he brought this up to her, she didn't know what his problem was. She felt there was nothing she could do there. Some people seem to be born without the empathy gene—but it is painful to live with them if you own one.

Sexual levels—both desire and imagination

This is tricky, because it's hard to know if you are well paired even if you've been having sex before you commit to each other. The problem is that in the beginning of a relationship almost everyone is a horny devil, but it is a few years of living together that sorts out the real sex enthusiasts from the ones who were merely enjoying a temporary boost from their adrenal glands.

So this argues for a deep investigation of how important sex really is to your partner, and here is an ironic twist: The best indication of the future is the past. In other words, your best bet is on someone who has had a lot of lovers or who lets you know that the ex was pretty damn good in bed (you hope he or she will say that was the only thing that kept them together because everything else was rotten, and that it was important to him or her). Because, guess what? If she or he has put up with a bad sex life in the past it's unlikely (though not unknown) that it will be very important to her or him in the future.

Now if you are no sex kitten/stud muffin yourself, just be honest with yourself about what you want and look for someone with approximately that level of sexual intensity and curiosity. Because believe me, if you've got someone who is way more interested and far-out than you are it can become a burden and a growth medium for anger. Conversely if you are the person who dreams of being tied up, making love in doorways, and can't go to sleep without at least one orgasm, you are going to be pretty disappointed in what you have to settle for.

Additional characteristics to think about

I have mentioned a few things that might really be important to consider: similar passion about life, the ability to empathize with another person, a similar amount of energy, and a similar approach to sex. There are a few other things that are important and aren't myths—at least I don't think they are. Let me state the ones that seem to wear well.

The same goals in life

You can't end up together if you are not going to the same place. It is extremely important that you both agree on what kind of lifestyle you want. Does it take money? Will it require sacrificing precious time with each other to get there? Or are you ambitious in other ways? Do you both want to see as much of the world, as soon as you can, even if it is in a tent, forever? There are no right answers here—only matched answers count. Love can make you kid yourself—you can say money doesn't matter, or that you can put away your travel dreams for this person who is so devastatingly important to you now . . . but I think those longings come back. Moreover, while goals can change, more often they do not. Long-term relationships work best when there is a mutual dedication to do what it takes to get you where you both want to go. Sometimes you start out on the same path and someone leaves it. That can't be helped. But it helps a lot to start out in the same direction and at the same speed.

Collaborative skills

You'd better pick someone who "works and plays well with others." Because no matter what else you have going for you as a couple, someone who can't collaborate is not going to go the distance. The trouble could be arrogance, or insensitivity, or narcissism, or just being a spoiled brat. It doesn't really matter what the cause is; you really need someone who has the ability to know you both are on the same team— and it will take being a team to put together a good life.

Generosity

There will be times when one person has to give more than the other. One person could be sick, or out of a job, or wildly successful and needs some back up. Some partners have the ability to give more under such circumstances and some don't. They get resentful quickly because being generous doesn't give them pleasure, they feel taken advantage of. Granted, things can't stay out of balance too long—it is hard for most of us to stay generous indefinitely. But there will be sustained periods when this will be necessary, and this is a trait that is badly needed.

Respect

Each person has values that have to be lived up to. And if a partner can't fulfill those expectations, the foundation of that relationship disintegrates. It may be attached to earning a living, or behaving honorably under duress, or being able to handle children with wisdom and restraint. Everyone has his or her own list of what makes a person worthy of respect. One reason most people need to take time to know each other before they make a commitment is to find out if someone meets their standard of respect, because if respect isn't there, contempt will eventually invade and destroy the ability to love that person. Unfortunately, when we are in love, we are romantically and hormonally unbalanced and we often gloss over the cues that tell us there are things about this person that do not live up to our values. The only safety net here is to let the most passionate part of the relationship subside before commitments are made. But some people just can't wait.

Similar intelligence

This one seems to be more important for women than for men—although, ultimately, I think it is important for both members of the couple—and becomes more and more important over the life cycle of the relationship. When you are young and overwhelmed with each other's face, body, and personality, intelligence seems a given—and having a partner whom you can use as a counselor and decision maker on a par with yourself is taken for granted. But as life's challenges come down the line (and just plain old everyday issues need to be taken on), having a partner who makes bad choices or whose judgment is off usually diminishes loving feelings.

A future orientation

This is one that I don't see mentioned often, but it seems to me that it is maybe the most important thing you can want in a partner—someone who lives for the present and future, not in the past. Many people have had a traumatic childhood, suffered serious bouts of illness, or endured grave losses of loved ones. It's the name of this game we call life.

But some people get stuck in what they have lost, missed, or been abused by—and others stay fixated on the good, the better, the future, the possibility of joy. Optimism and the determination to be happy might be the best things a partner can offer in any long-term relationship.

Bottom line

Figuring out what is important in a partner is more of an art form than a science. Not that it isn't the subject of thousands of hours of behavioral scientists' careers; of course it is and should be. But while research can tell you a great deal about statistical probabilities of divorce and give you new ways to better understand human personality and interaction, the process of pairing is ultimately a decision you make in partnership with your brain, body, and feelings Once you have picked someone to zero in on, there really is a lot in the relationship literature to help you conduct and repair your relationship better. But picking that person is the most momentous part of the process, and no one can tell you exactly whom to choose. All I am saying is to think broadly and honestly about the things that make a life worth living with someone and question some of the traditional rules. Yesterday's statistics do not have to be tomorrow's. Look deeply into yourself and know what is most important to you personally. You may have an unexpected romance that could turn out to be just right for you.

7

MYTH:

Pick someone who has sown her or his wild oats and is now ready to settle down with you

Fathers used to advise their sons, and now quite a few mothers tell their daughters: "Go out and sow your wild oats before you settle down." (It was a more agricultural time when this advice was first coined.) And then, so the advice went, you will have had your fill of being a wild thing and will be able to settle down to more orderly hoeing and tilling. Or you should pick someone who has now seen the world and is ready to settle down with you.

A lot of young people are heeding this advice, and there is certainly a lot of oat sowing going on. The vast majority of American and Western European young people are not virgins when they marry; the mean age of marriage is now moving up into the late twenties, and a bit of experience not only doesn't damage a person's marriagability— it enhances it. The single lifestyle is a sexually active lifestyle.

Now, I would be the last person to say this is a bad thing. I look back at the late sixties and seventies with extreme fondness. Of course, getting some sexual experience is a lot of fun. But the problem is stopping, or stopping in time for your first or second marriage. In fact, the research indicates that the best predictor of nonmonogamy after marriage is how much premarital sex there has been before it. What should this tell us? I think it should tell us one of four things:

1. If monogamy is the most important thing to you in a relationship, you have a better chance of finding it if you find someone who did not have a lot of premarital sex.

2. If someone had a lot of premarital sex you better allow a little bit of slack—you are probably going to need it.

3. Since we are all creatures of habit, better not engage in an intense sexual tour of a variety of lovers if you don't want to keep it up.

4. And, at the very least, if you want to keep yourself—or someone else with a wild sexual past—pleased and loyal, you'd better keep up a very high standard of sexual innovation and intensity.

I know this is going against common wisdom and the lifestyle many of you are already leading; but thinking about how your present sexual life will affect your sexuality after you are committed to someone is at least worth considering. What you like may be hard to give up, even when you want to.

Jennifer, for example, is in love with Alvaro. They are well matched in a number of ways. They are both twenty-four, adventurous, and attractive. They met each other at a gym where they both worked as physical fitness instructors. They admired each other's work and facility with clients and decided to become a team: now they lead classes together and have just produced their first video. They try not to be apart and when they travel with their work they have been clever about finding great places to teach together in wonderful settings, like cruise ships and resorts. Both of them say they are having a great time, but Alvaro would like to settle down in one place. He would like to become a father. Jennifer, although she is sure she is in love with Alvaro, just can't imagine that she can be the kind of wife and mother that he wants, which is to say, faithful.

She says, "I am having a great time with Alvaro. I think if he and I had met ten years from now, it would be perfect. But to tell you the truth, I can't see Alvaro as the last guy I will ever sleep with. Not that I have eyes for anyone else but him right now. I don't. But I know my history. I am a very physical person. I am a very curious person. I've gotten to know people by having sex with them, and I am just not ready to say there will never be another one." She is honest with Alvaro, which drives him crazy. He won't make any bargain that includes nonmonogamy, but he loves Jennifer so they stay together. It is a standoff.

♥

Sometimes, however, the recognition that a person is wedded to a nonmonogamous lifestyle comes *after* a marriage. Lincoln was a man with very little sexual experience. He had married his high school sweetheart two years after they graduated, and they were married for twelve years. It would never have even crossed his mind to be unfaithful. The marriage had its ups and downs, but he was surprised when his wife told him she wanted a divorce. He thought it was "plenty good enough" and didn't understand her complaints about not being "free to be me" while married to him. She left rather suddenly, and although she was good about property settlement and visitation with their son, he was bitter. He was also nervous. He had never really been a single man, and he was not comfortable dating. But he signed up for some singles dating clubs and dutifully started making lunch dates. On one of these dates he met Frieda. Frieda was exactly the kind of woman he had never been attracted to in high school—wild, nonconformist, sexy. But she was also warm and funny, and he liked being with her. She was a crafts person like him; he made furniture, she had a frame shop and did high-quality matting and personally crafted frames. They got on

better and better and when they made love, he felt it was more exciting than it had ever been with his wife. As soon as he felt it was a serious relationship, he told Frieda that if they were going to keep seeing
each other, she had to be monogamous.

Frieda balked at the idea. She had been on her own since high school
and had had many lovers. She told him this would be hard for her, but
she would try. She did try and they married. But as they years wore on,
Frieda couldn't hold up her end of the bargain. She wasn't out of love
with Lincoln; she simply was a woman of capacious appetites. She confided in our interview that while she is true to Lincoln "in her way,"
she is not true in a way that Lincoln would appreciate. She is very fear-
ful that he will find out someday because she loves him and she thinks
they are very well suited to each other in other respects. "Lincoln
thinks that just because we love each other I am a totally different person. But I'm not. But it's just like a man. They think once you are
'theirs,' you are a new person." Frieda sounds cocky when she says this,
but she really doesn't want her marriage to break up over the issue of
fidelity; yet she is unable to resist an occasional fling.

Is this sexual addiction? That seems to be the chic sexual problem of
the last decade of the twentieth century, and perhaps now it will continue into the twenty-first. I don't think it is addiction in the strict form
of that word. There is no physiological and chemical craving that will
give you the shakes if you don't have sex with a new person. I think it
is more learned behavior, and more and more of us have learned to love
the hormonal charge of conquering a new person or unveiling a new
body.

But let's say that in your case, or in the case of your honey, the desire
is to be monogamous because experience has taught you that nonmonogamy has a tendency to wreck relationships and you are tired of
blowing up marriages and commitments. Then you might take into account the last fact that I mentioned, that someone who has sown a lot
of wild oats is likely to know one oat from the other, and is looking for
a high-quality product. If you are going to be with someone who is

sexually experienced, you had better take a postgraduate course in sexual imagination because the chances are she or he is not going to be satisfied by "vanilla" sex. Does this mean you have to buy a rack or a trapeze? Not usually. But it does mean that someone who liked sex before is going to like it now and that sex is not going to be back-burnered in this relationship.

♥

Uli, a writer and a guy who loves sex, intended to make it a part of every day of his life but Gretchen, his wife, sees things differently. When I talked to him, he was about to part from his wife of six years (and partner for four years before that) because of their differences about sex. "When we first met it was wild: on the table, in the kitchen, on the porch, anywhere we could get our hands on each other. It was like that for all four years we lived together, and she had been a party girl before that so I thought I knew what I was getting. But it's like a bad joke. As soon as we got married, no, as soon as we had Priscilla (their daughter), my sex kitten turned into a lazy, indifferent cat!"

When Uli's wife told him that she really thought he was adolescent about sex and when she got angry that he was pressuring her every day, the relationship went into the deep freeze. Uli thought of extramarital affairs, but he couldn't bring himself to do something like that and he kept the marriage going longer than he wanted to because he did not want to live separately from his daughter. But after a while he just couldn't stand it. He said their sex life had to get better or he was leaving. His wife resolutely stuck to her own preferences and told him to "grow up." That was the last straw, he is now living alone, and they are both talking to lawyers.

♥

Some people don't care. Sex isn't the center of their life. It's really no big deal. But for others, it is at the core of their identity. Some medical researchers think that there may be more than habit to explain this.

They believe there are high-testosterone types and low ones. Men have more testosterone than women, of course, but according to this theory, "high-T" women have a higher ratio of testosterone to estrogen than other women—and a little bit of T in women goes a long way. Clinicians and researchers who believe in the hormone theory of sexual appetite think that when people fall in love and in lust they have a temporary boost to their endocrine system that is brought on by the action of phenylethylamine (PEA), a naturally occurring substance that acts like amphetamines in the body and that is produced during infatuation. In other words, when you are attracted to someone, your brain is flooded with its own "speed," which is why you are higher than a kite.

This makes for a very deceptive presentation of self, because even people who usually don't have much sexual interest are turned on and sexually aggressive during this period. When their sexual interest is stoked by relationship uncertainty, any suitor can look like a sexual athlete. But once security and everyday life pacify this hormonalized state of mind, the "sex kitten" disappears.

So here is another reason to judge people from their past performances and not from proximal information. If they've "never felt this way before, never acted this way before," they may never act that way again! And for those people to whom sex is as much a part of their life as eating and sleeping, this is bad news. People who have "sown their wild oats" are telling you a lot about themselves—don't think of it is as unimportant. And if it's you, be true to yourself, and to what you promise others.

8

MYTH:
It is flattering to have a jealous lover

Sure there are nice kinds of jealousy: That first moment when your girl shows that she cares if you go out with someone else. When he calls, you're not there, and he's miffed and worried. Those are sweet moments of recognition: I love her; he needs me. A little bit of jealousy has its purposes, but a lot of it is useless and sometimes dangerous. What I don't understand is no matter how many stalker, control-freak movies some women see, they still tolerate excessive jealousy from a boyfriend or husband. No matter how many times a man has seen movies in which jealous women go beserk, he is rather flattered when his girlfriend tells him that if he is ever unfaithful she will shoot him. Maybe you feel the same way? Then I would like to ask you a question: "Which part of *psychosis* do you not understand?"

Let me tell you a story of someone I know who started out thinking her fiancé's attentions were wonderful and found out that they were just part of a deeper set of emotional problems. When Eileen met Ross in graduate school, she loved his courtly attentions. She was tired of guys who went "dutch," who showed up unshaven, who, in general, didn't seem to put any effort into showing that they cared about how she felt. Ross was completely different. He came from a wealthy family, had been to prep schools, and had a certain style in everything he did. The day before their first date, he had a dozen roses delivered to her apartment. When he arrived, he had a small gift for her—a sachet. He had made a couple of dinner reservations so that she could pick the one she liked best. She was completely charmed.

He was no less attentive as time wore on. In fact, he cared a lot about details. He would ask what she was wearing and bring a rose to match. He remembered dates that were important to both of them. If she was having a test or paper due, he would plan their evening so that she could study. She felt taken care of. For six months things seemed perfect, and then the first tiny indication of something going wrong appeared after they got engaged. They were at a formal party, and she had worn a pretty, sexy dress—nothing low cut but a long dress that hugged her body. When he saw her in it, he said, "Are you going out in public in that dress?" She was surprised. The dress fit her body, but it had a turtleneck top and went down to the floor. She thought that perhaps she had misunderstood and that the party was more informal than she thought. She asked him if that were so. He said no, it was formal, but didn't she think she was calling too much attention to herself? She got a bit huffy and said no, and he shrugged and backed off. But all evening, she felt uneasy in a way she didn't like. Still, she didn't think about it all that much. He didn't say much more that evening at the party.

However, later, back at her apartment, the issue of how she had dressed came back again. They talked about it for at least an hour. And then, a couple of days later, he brought it up again. He thought she dressed to get "male attention." She got angry and told him to cut it out.

After that there was a series of incidents, the worst of which was at a dinner party where he accused her of spending too much time talking to her dinner partner and asked if the man had asked her out. Again, she was amazed and told him, laughingly, that yes, they had made a date to go to London. He became red in the face and angry. He then called her a whore. "That's when I knew that this was not right, that he had a problem. Up to then I have to admit that I kind of enjoyed his possessiveness, his idea that every man in the world wanted me. I hadn't been wanted that much before by anyone, and I thought it was proof of how much he loved me. But when he got paranoid about my running off with this geek I was having dinner with, I knew that I was in over my head. I was really sad that this wasn't going to work out; everyone in my family thought I had made the catch of the century. Maybe that's why I tried to ignore all the earlier signs of what turned out to be his obsessive need to control my actions."

Eileen said it was over, that he didn't trust her and she didn't like worrying about it. He apologized and sent flowers the next day. But by that time Eileen knew something was wrong with him and wanted out, even though her family and friends were telling her to give him another chance. They saw it her way, however, when after a couple of more days of sending her poems and flowers to no avail, he came over to her apartment and tried to break the door down. "I felt terrible," said Eileen. "But I had to call the police and had to fill out a report. I hated getting him in that kind of trouble. He was in law school, and that pretty much was the end of it. But by that time I had reason to be scared, so scared that I had a restraining order. He even violated that a couple of times, but thank God his family stepped in and sent him somewhere." These kinds of stories are not rare—but jealousy doesn't have to go this far to tell you that you are with the wrong person. In fact, in general, anything but a little bit of jealousy tells you a lot, all of it bad.

♥

Think about what jealousy is really telling you about your relationship:

They don't trust you

You know it's not a compliment if someone calls you late at night and jumps to conclusions. If he is upset that you don't answer at four in the morning, he should be worrying about your life, not your sex organs. If you two have a commitment, he should assume that you are sticking to that, or if there is no understanding between you, and there should be, well, that can be worked out too.

On the other hand, maybe you have made it clear that you are not ready to be tied down, and where you are at four a.m. is your business. If you have been clear, it is the other person's obligation either to accept that and get over worrying about it, or drop the relationship and find someone who is on the same page he or she is. What is not cool is being in a relationship with stated premises and having them questioned all the time. This is a massive waste of energy, and the no-confidence vote is an insult. Sometimes it is just crazy. I knew a woman, who ultimately became a nun, who was, as you can imagine, the most trustworthy virginal woman in the known world. She met this guy who seemed to be afraid that she would be sleeping with the NFL if she wasn't in his sight all the time. She really was a virgin! She tolerated this craziness until he kept accusing her of things almost daily. He was her first love and her last.

Most stories are not this dramatic, but the principle is the same: If someone is very jealous, his or her attitude is a statement in and of itself—it questions your truthfulness. And to what end is this insulting imputation made? If you are the kind of person who would lie, and your partner doesn't like that, he or she is free to leave. Casting doubt doesn't help. On the other hand, if you are telling the truth, your partner is demeaning both of you and the relationship. In either case, it's a no-win tactic.

They don't believe in themselves

When you love someone, and he says he loves you, you should believe that what he says is true unless there is proof positive to the contrary. Better to be wrong, however, than to doubt it. That doesn't mean you should be a chump (for example, not questioning why he can't ever see you on Saturday nights . . .), but it does mean that you should believe you are worth loving, and why would anyone take a chance of losing you?

Jealous people are insecure people. That might be hard for you to believe. Your jealous lover might seem to be, in your opinion, brighter, better-looking, and more successful than anyone else you can think of. But she might not feel that way. She might feel that you are the best thing that ever happened to her and that's why she holds on so tight. Reassure her, but remember, if she is not capable of backing off, then something deeper and harder to change might be at the core of her personality. And someone that insecure would not be a picnic to live with.

They might be control freaks

Both of the case studies that I have included in this chapter are about men that had to control their women. Their jealousy was both a symptom and a method. A jealous woman might use a different approach than a man; for example, she is less likely to use physical force or violent threats. She is probably more likely to say that she will hurt herself if you leave her. But make no mistake about it, laments of "You don't love me" or "You had me worried" or "Have you called that woman you were talking to last week at the party?" are all control maneuvers. Sure, they show the person is very much interested in you, but these kind of manipulative moves also show that this person is going to try to control your actions rather than trust who you are and what you do. A little bit of this is normal. Many people get insecure from time to time and try to pin their partner down. But normal people eventually relax as they get affection and time. Someone who can never be reassured, who can't take you at your word, is different; this kind of person will want to control you even when he or she is dead sure of you.

They might be dangerous

I don't have to beat this theme into the ground—both of the vignettes I've given could have turned even uglier. You know you can listen in on any TV news in any town and there is usually a story about a divorced husband who killed his ex-wife because she was dating someone else and he couldn't stand it. The Medea story happens as well. The ancient Greek play is based on the horrific capacity of some women (and men) to punish a partner who jilted them by killing their mutual children. I wish these things didn't exist, but they do. Stay away from a person who is very jealous.

Here are some cues to know if the person you are with is outside the bounds of reasonable insecurity.

They call and check in the middle of the night

It's one thing if they are calling just to be romantic, another if they want to see if you are home. After a while, you can tell the difference.

They grill your friends

Your friends start to show concern. At first, it sounds as if your partner is just madly in love with you and wants to hear stories about you.

But they go in deeper about old lovers, ex-husbands, and they obsess about them—in fact, there is a compulsive aspect to their digging for details. If it makes you uneasy, listen to that feeling.

They are hostile to old lovers

What's over is over. They should feel generous; after all, these people lost out (whether you broke up with them or they broke up with you!). But your new love bristles in the presence of old lovers or gets upset if you even talk to someone you used to go out with. A little awkwardness is understandable, maybe even a little bit of jealousy at having had to share you with anyone. But this person is supposed to be a grown-up and so are you. If he wants someone without a past, it probably isn't you. And quite honestly, if a person is really jealous, he could be jealous about anyone: siblings, friends, dogs. It's not about logic and it's not about love.

They go through your things

A lot of people have done this when they felt insecure, maybe suspected their partner was cheating on them (and maybe were right). Almost everyone has weak moments in his or her life and investigates a suspicion. We can't expect ourselves or someone else to be perfectly secure. But jealousy is not flattering, and detective work like rummaging through pockets (whether it's you or a partner who is trespassing on privacy) is definitely something that shouldn't happen again. If you think your things are being rifled through, something is wrong with the relationship. If you are doing something that a reasonable person would be worried or jealous about, you should deal with it, but deal with the investigative snooping too. No relationship can tolerate this.

They don't just threaten you; they say they would kill themselves if they lost you

This is probably self-explanatory. Certainly the threats to you are! But don't overlook the threats of self-destruction. It's not fair; it's a control tactic, and it's not sweet or touching. Tell them to get some help.

On the other hand, if you really are an artist at arousing insecurities, you need to stop it. It's only fair to do the following quick check to see what *you* might be doing that would turn a reasonable person into a jealous lover. If any of these fit, cut it out!

Being a hot-and-cold lover

This is a great way to get someone addicted to you if he or she is interested at all. But it can go too far and make someone so insecure that everything seems like a threat to the relationship. You come on strong, then you are unreachable (literally or emotionally). You are hot one day, promising the sun and the moon, and then the next you put your old lover's picture back up. In other words, you are totally inconsistent—when you are good, you are great. And then it's as if you are attached to your honey by the slenderest of threads. This is going to make someone awfully insecure and jealous, if he or she is attached enough to stick around. Think about whether this is a fair way to conduct a relationship and if you really want to do this to someone you care about.

Too much secrecy

You are so used to your independence and privacy that you won't even tell someone when you are going to the bakery. You really do like to walk your dog at three a.m., but you don't mention that to your honey, who is calling you and wondering who you are with. In other words, you don't feel as though you owe anyone an explanation—and maybe you don't. But then don't be surprised when you get jealous reactions, which can ruin a perfectly promising relationship.

You never check in

You don't understand your sweetheart's jealousy because when you are there you are one hundred percent present, full of reassuring comments. She or he should know how you feel. But you travel a lot and you never call. You never call in between the times you are present. Most partners need intermediate reinforcement. And if you give it, it will solve a lot of problems.

You don't explain your need for privacy

If you are with a person who is very gregarious, your lover might not be able to understand that some people actually want some time alone. If you are an introvert, this may not be a good match anyhow. But if there are other things that make you a good match, you can save your sweetheart a lot of worry by convincing him that when you say you want to be alone, it has nothing to do with him and everything with how you get your equilibrium and strength. If you can explain this, he can stop taking it personally.

Tell them they are the only one (if they are)

This is one of those places where honesty really helps. If there are other people, let her know and she will either live with it or she won't. If there is no one else, however, don't withhold that information just to keep the upper hand or to keep your options open (your options are always open until you agree to close them). Give this person the reassurance you can. If your lover is still jealous after that, don't be flattered; look elsewhere. Jealousy should be a fleeting phase in a good relationship. It is a myth that it makes anything better.

9

MYTH:
You should never have sex on the first date

Most books written by a sex counselor, family sociologist, or popular writer tell women to wait quite a while before having sex with a date. Make him know and respect you first, they say, or he will lose respect for you, use you, and leave you. He will want to get you in bed as soon as he can, but if he is successful, he will conclude you are "too easy" and, therefore, not be appropriate for a long-term partner (never mind that by this same logic, he isn't worth much either).

A lot of women didn't like that double standard, and in the late sixties and seventies tried to toss it out. Many found that most of the time the double standard was tougher than they were. They really didn't enjoy one night of passion and no call back the next day. Maybe it worked for the guys, but for women, a great night felt as if it should lead to at least a dating relationship. But I'll tell you something: There are more men these days who know that a good bed partner is hard to find—and that there is nothing wrong with an adventurous female. In fact, the double standard has been reduced (though, I admit, it has not disappeared) and there are plenty of guys out there who don't back away after sex just because a woman is available right away. She is acting on her instincts, just as he is acting on his. Sex is important for her, as it is for him. It's a way to say, "Who are you? Hmmm. Maybe someone I want to know better."

Of course, *The Rules* and other throwback books catering to women's fears of not being wanted and married say that this is a no-no. But I think, in some cases, they are wrong. In fact, hot sex early on *can* be a shortcut to commitment. Why should you believe me? Well, let me give you some good reasons and then some case studies. If you are still interested, I'll tell you how to know if you can do this and, if you can, how to do it right—and, of course, I'll give you the downside. Here are some reasons to forget the "not on the first night" rule:

Sometimes the moment is perfect

There are magical moments, and you ignore them at your peril. It's easy to get jaded in this era of manufactured romance and quick and short couplings. Still, rule number one—and two and three—is trust your gut. If there is something special happening, then don't ignore it. Many meetings only present one chance—second chances are even rarer than any chance at all.

If everything fits together, then let it proceed as it should. It is a great gift to begin anything right. One woman who married her "first-date fling" told me, "He picked me up and looked great. For some reason, I felt like I looked better than I had in years. He brought me freesias, which are my favorite flowers in the world, and getting those on the first date melted my heart. We went to a restaurant where I think I had the best dinner of my life. The night was balmy, and the stars were so perfect they looked like someone had brushed them up for this evening. When he kissed me, I knew that I wanted to keep this going all night long. We did and the sex was equally special. Both of us think of that night as enchanted." Sure, it could have ended right there for her, but it didn't. Both of these people took advantage of a passionate romantic moment, and it began a relationship.

Sometimes you only get one chance

Wise people always say take your time (there will always be another chance) or don't rush things (good things take time to grow). There is a lot of truth to that, and probably nothing but time tells you certain things: someone's true character, long-term compatibility, important core revelations, and so forth. But sometimes, you get only one chance. You are on vacation and if the impression isn't made, it won't be made at all. The person might be deciding whether or not to go back to her partner, and there is this little window of time when she is "on the market." You might be in an airport in a city for one day, and you are talking to someone who is so great you can't believe your luck. You get the picture. Under ordinary circumstances, you have time to develop something; but under these circumstances, you have a matter of minutes or hours.

Is that too Hollywoodish? I don't think so. If you don't have time working for you—you'd better have hormones. And even more than hormones, you need guts. It is scary to chance not only total rejection—but also maybe even anger if you move too fast and the person feels insulted, rather than complimented. Still, nothing ventured, nothing gained. Or, to keep using old and very true sayings: *carpe diem*— seize the day (or the night).

Always show off your best qualities

It may be that you have a hidden talent—you are great in bed. You know how to make a woman glow from head to toe, or you know that foreplay is the whole game. Or you are a woman who knows how to make a man feel as if he were sixteen again—well, what he wanted to be when he was sixteen. These are not small talents. In my book, this is the equivalent of mentioning you have earned the Pulitzer Prize (unhappily no prizes are awarded for this kind of talent, but that doesn't mean they shouldn't be!). If you wait too long, you may never get to reveal this aspect of your personality. This is fine most of the time— you don't want unworthy people to experience your artistry. But when you come upon someone fascinating who may not have guessed yet how special you are—it's time to unveil yourself. There is more than one surprised partner who took a new look because this passionate, knowledgeable person just knocked his or her socks off, and of course everything else that follows.

Some men will never open up unless it's sexual

Sad but true. Hormones course through everyone's bodies, but men seem to need a sexual experience more than women to "get in touch with their inner child." If you both don't go to sleep afterward (a big if) or if there is some time between lovemaking bouts, there will be a chance for real conversation about the self, life, who you are, who he or she is.

Men and women are, of course, somewhat different about conversation during and after sex. Women use sexuality to express their feelings, and men use sex to retrieve them. It's been said that when women love someone it is arousing to them and if they are just plain aroused, they may justify it by thinking it must be love. Men are quite the opposite—they think sex is sex—and yet still what starts out as physical can be a catalyst for letting out deeper feelings and, perhaps, create love. In long-term relationships, both men and women use sex to bridge emotional gaps. Sex is a way to get past petty details and daily distractions. So what makes you think it can't work that way right off the bat? I think it does, at least for some people.

Sex early on can lead to quicker self-disclosure and intimacy

You know how long it can take sometimes to really get down to feelings, and what you both want and expect from a relationship. Granted, there is a lot to be said for developing a friendship slowly, so you know exactly what someone is made of and you know that neither of you will hurt the other. I have nothing against this kind of relationship. A love affair based on a friendship feels safe, solid, comfortable, and deep. But you have to be the patient sort.

However, if you are an A type like me, it isn't going to happen that way—at least not most of the time. You want to know immediately what there is to know and to see if it's worth your time. For brave A types (and I do mean brave—see my last section here about the downside) sex is the perfect answer. You are in quickly and you may be out quickly, but you get a lot of information and if you both really like it, you could be on your way to seeing what this relationship can be in record time. But don't just take my word for this. Here are a couple of case studies.

Mimi had agreed to meet her girlfriend for a week at a resort. She had been stressed-out at work, and she was blue about the loss of her longtime boyfriend. She had really thought this one would work out and had done everything in her power to do everything right. They had met on a company "team building" project and had respected each other's contributions. Over time, they got to know each other well, and she was pleased and excited when he asked her out to lunch. There was a lot of mutual attraction at that lunch, but she kept her cards to herself. They went out six months before things got really passionate. They slept with each other after a good deal of discussion, and the evening was wonderful. But somehow she couldn't get Roger to commit. They had been going out for two years before she realized he just wasn't in love with her. She finally found the nerve to back out of the relationship, but she felt tired and depressed. When Alice, her close friend from school, suggested a holiday, she took the invitation seriously and they went.

Nothing is ever perfect, though, and their plane was delayed because both the originating airport and their destination airport were fogged in. The airline gave them food coupons and they went to use them at a restaurant. It was full of passengers who also had coupons, and people had to double up on seating. They found themselves seated next to a couple of guys who were on the same flight, and they swapped gripes. One of the guys was darling. They had a lot of fun talking to each other and she could see that Alice was giving her that "No, you don't!" look, and she certainly didn't intend to get involved with anyone. But she was in a holiday mood and when she found out that this guy was on a golfing trip, it occurred to her that maybe she could see him while she was on the vacation. But things went faster than that. He asked her to sit with him on the plane when it finally took off and, during the course of the plane ride, they got turned on. She let him kiss her and touch her and was amazed at her own boldness. They agreed to meet at his hotel after the plane landed. Alice was flabbergasted when Mimi told her the plan. She told her it was completely out of character, was "cheap," and would make her feel lousy afterwards. But Mimi didn't care. She was in the mood to break rules.

So, after they unpacked, Mimi took a cab over to the resort where this guy, Sam, was staying. He was quite the experienced seducer. They went swimming first, and afterward he slowly wiped her off, head to toe. She thought to herself, "I'm just going to enjoy this. This guy does this a lot, and I'm just going to have a good time."

The evening was wildly passionate—Sam really did know what he was doing and in the morning, when she woke up, she had to admit she really hated to have this as a one-time-only event. Having nothing to lose, she told him that and asked if he wanted to get together the next night. After making all the usual protestations about not being ready for a relationship, he said he did want to see her after his day with his golfing buddies. To make a long week short—they saw each other every night and at the end of the week he looked at her and said, "This isn't just about sex, is it?" They saw each other back in the city when they returned—and a year and a half later they were living together. They both consider the relationship serious and hope that it will work out.

Now, of course this could have been just a week of delusions and tropical breezes. But their sexual relationship gave them time to talk, get to know each other, and be more intimate more quickly than a traditional "dating" relationship would have. It could have been a "false intimacy" if either of them had been cynical or manipulative. But they were both open to the deeper possibilities that occurred because of their sexual attraction.

♥

Here's another example:

Garrit had been married for thirteen years when his wife told him she'd been having an affair and was leaving. He was devastated and furious. He had been perfectly faithful even though he'd had plenty of chances not to be. Their relationship had had problems, but he always assumed that they would work them out because they had to. They had both promised each other a lifetime commitment, and it never occurred to him that there could be an ending to it. When he was out of the relationship for two weeks, he thought to himself, "I was meant to be married. I don't want to date. I don't like games. What am I was supposed to do?"

Garrit is that rare man that all women hope for and few find: extremely good-looking and totally unaware of it. He is tall and striking, and women are very attracted to him. But, two weeks out of the marriage, he felt lost. Then, one night at a party, he met what might be thought of as his exact opposite. Amanda was a party girl. She had been out of her own marriage for eight years and was independent and nonchalant. As she puts it: "At that time of my life, my expectations were a good night, nothing more." She thought Garrit was very attractive and they spent the party talking to each other, then went out afterward to get something to eat. They kept talking all night and, in the morning, went back to his place and made love. Garrit thought it was great, but he was so nervous he could hardly do anything. "Still, I knew that if Amanda and I were going to be anything, and I felt like I wanted us to be something, I couldn't pretend to do this impersonal sex thing." He told her that if she wanted to see him, she had to stop seeing other guys right away!

Amanda was startled. She was used to easy beginnings and quick endings. But Garrit was the kind of guy who had two speeds: Go and Stop. He was on Go, and Amanda made a quick decision: to treat this like a relationship, stop seeing other people, and get to know Garrit. They moved in with each other in six weeks, lived together for two years, and have been married for eighteen. Sometimes things start suddenly—and last.

The downside

Anything this quick can be dangerous, literally and psychologically. If you meet a complete psychopath at a bar, he probably isn't going to be wearing a sign saying "I am lethal." The less you know about someone, the more risk there is about getting intimate very quickly. You can't dismiss this possibility, and for most women this is enough of a deal breaker that unless a guy is vetted by a friend or acquaintance, the risk is too great. But even beyond personal safety, there are these considerations:

The person who treats you like disposable tissue

You guessed wrong. Sex on the first date turned out to be sex on the last date. No fun—particularly if you thought the evening was terrific and you want more. But now the person crosses the street to avoid you. Your only defense is to tell her she is being a big baby and that she doesn't have to be frightened of you. Furthermore, she shouldn't do this sort of thing if she can't handle it. But that's pretty lame if what you really wanted was more, not less, of her.

The person who starts planning the wedding the next morning

This can be even more upsetting than losing someone. You wanted a beginning, but this wasn't supposed to be a wedding night. The person seemed lighthearted and playful enough, but the hormones she is percolating turn out to be oxytocin—those that mothers produce when they bond with their babies. In the worst case, you can get a "stalker," which comes in both male and female form. In the slightly less than worst case, the person who you thought could just experiment with you has now translated this into a promise of "Big Things" and you are cast in the role of creep or slut and/or player or whatever. No fun, particularly if he or she smears your name around the office.

Pregnancy: An "accident" with the wrong person

Any time you share your body with someone, you have the possibility of sharing your DNA. If you don't use contraception, and even if you do, accidents happen. And not everybody feels that an abortion is the answer. If you are the guy, you could be in big trouble because you cannot control your partner's decision. If you are the woman and cannot bring yourself to have an abortion, you now will have a child with someone you don't know. This is not theoretical. I have a friend who had one night of passion with a lovely stranger and now is the father of twins with a mother he still doesn't know any better than the night he spent with her. It doesn't help at all that she hates him and does everything she can to block his visitation with his kids. Remember: Unintended fertility is not a rare occurrence. This could definitely crunch your life.

Sexual diseases and that sort of thing

Ditto on sexually transmitted diseases. Condoms may protect well against HIV and a few other diseases when the infection is passed through the semen or blood—but plenty of diseases are contracted by mere skin contact and some of those diseases, herpes and HPV, for example, are forever. The more people you sleep with, the better your chances of encountering one of these less-than-erotic microbes or viruses. You might want to reserve spontaneous sex on a first meeting for an extremely compelling person.

Great at dinner and a bust in bed

Okay—this person is so fine that, although you are normally conservative, you opt for sudden sex. However, this person who looked so sexy at dinner that it hurt turned into an iceberg in bed—immovable enough to wreck any vessel. Now you are stuck with someone you don't really know *and* the sex is pitiful. You can chalk it up to bad luck, but it's no fun—and it is hard to say, in the middle of a sexual encounter, "Uh, could we just forget this and go to a movie?" Etiquette requires that you do not let your untalented partner know how disappointed you are and because it isn't a relationship, you can't really make it any better. It's just one of those experiences that make you decide not to do this again.

Your child is reading this chapter

Funny how a lot of things sound just fine for oneself until you think of how it would be if your son or daughter was buying this philosophy. You know it's high risk, and you don't want your child in the arms of someone who doesn't love him or her. So I'll issue a caveat—you need to be a bit older to try this out. You have to have a lot of self-esteem, know when this is the right tack to take, and be able to protect yourself emotionally and physically.

A last piece of advice

This sexual philosophy has some good and bad points, and it's not for everyone. You have to know yourself and you might be the kind of person who has to be in love, and be sure you are loved, before you can enjoy sex or feel that you have lived up to your own moral standard. So be it. You have to be true to who you are. Furthermore, you have to trust your intuition about your partner. No matter how you feel, you might be with someone who needs a long, slow buildup. If you know that's who he is and that's what he wants, don't push it. Let intimacy build naturally through communication and small, steady increments of demonstrated affection. Lots of people have gotten serious (and become committed) using this model.

But at least think about what I've said here. There are moments in life, and there are people you will meet, when a heedless plunge into passion is exactly the thing to do and I'd hate for anyone to miss that opportunity! Is it risky? Absolutely. If you go to bed with someone shortly after you've begun to see her or him, you should be aware that either one of you could decide this was a bad idea—and you should be prepared to be a good sport about it. Be careful in all ways, but re-member that sometimes there are risks in life that pay off, and a great night really can be the beginning of the best relationship you will ever have. Few friends or professionals are going to back me up on this, but personal histories do not lie and there are a lot of people out there whose lifetime love affairs began just this way.

10

MYTH:
Even if sex isn't fantastic in the beginning, it can be fixed

laine fell in love with Kirby on the first date. She had seen him around campus and thought he was the most adorable boy she had ever laid eyes on. She used to fantasize about what it would be like to kiss and be held by him, and she'd invent whole dialogues they would have together. When he turned up in one of her classes, she uncharacteristically pushed to the front of the room and grabbed the seat next to him. She remembers: "I knew I had to create a friendship right away, so I had the right to sit next to him."

It was sophomore year in college, and eventually Kirby asked her to the Spring Fling, the end-of-the-year formal dance. "The lights were strung up on trees, it was a warm night, my shoulders were bare, and just being next to him made my skin tingle," says Elaine. There was plenty of chemistry—and when Kirby kissed her, softly and gently, she felt her emotions stir. She couldn't wait to move on to more intense lovemaking.

But Kirby came from a very religious home, and he did not believe that sex before marriage was morally defensible. As their dating went on, they got into heavy kissing, bodies grinding against each other, and he would touch her breasts. But when she would try to touch him under his pants, he would move away and say that they had to control themselves.

After two years of rather furtive petting, they got engaged and Elaine was the happiest young woman in the world. Her parents liked Kirby very much, she liked his family, and she felt they had similar values. Although she was not very religious, she admired and even envied his deep faith, and felt he would be a wonderful father when the time came to have a family. Kirby was deeply in love with her, and every one of her friends told her what a great couple they were.

One night, about four months before the wedding, Elaine and Kirby could contain themselves no longer. They did not intend to have intercourse and thought they could take their clothes off and "do everything but." However, the evening turned into something of a disaster. "I guess I just couldn't see the reason for waiting any longer. I had had one previous lover and I knew what it could be like, and I couldn't bear not making love with Kirby. So I got him super turned-on, and his behavior shocked me. He grabbed my breasts so hard that it was painful, and he kissed me too hard and it hurt my mouth. I felt almost raped. He didn't mean to do that; it was just his way of being passionate. He didn't touch me to arouse me except a little bit, and that was rough too. I turned off and I felt bruised and had to just endure it. We both felt embarrassed and guilty—he for having sex and me for maneuvering him into this situation and having it all go wrong. We decided not to try again until after the wedding. The whole incident worried me, but I figured if the love was there, you could always work the sex out."

But that didn't turn out to be the case. Their wedding night was not much better and even months later, Elaine found herself flinching when Kirby would touch her during lovemaking. One night she decided to be totally honest with him about what felt good and what didn't. Kirby was not too defensive and told her to show him how to touch her. "This was the toughest of all," said Elaine. "I didn't really want to be my husband's teacher but it looked like that was the way it had to be. So I lay back and had him touch me more lightly and go where I told him to go. It was better. But it wasn't great."

Kirby listened and he really tried. He knew he wasn't a talented lover. He had feared as much when he was younger and felt so awkward with girls that he had backed away from them even though he was attractive and many young women had pursued him. He did everything that Elaine asked but when he got excited, he never felt that he really could synchronize her needs and his own. He came very quickly once he entered her and knew she didn't have an orgasm during intercourse, and that she even felt frustrated when he tried to give her an orgasm touching her clitoris. Finally they agreed that she would use a vibrator and he would just kiss her while she brought herself to orgasm. The only thing he wouldn't do for her was to have oral sex. It didn't appeal to him and, he confessed, once he had tried it, it appealed to him even less.

After five years Elaine had trouble getting Kirby to make love at all, and she was really upset. "So I said we needed to go to a sex therapist. Kirby didn't want to go at all, but I talked him into it. But I had no idea about how to pick out a sex therapist, and the person we got right out of the yellow pages didn't have a very good rapport with us. We went about four times, and then it just seemed ridiculous so we stopped."

The marriage went on for five more years. Right after their tenth anniversary, however, Elaine decided that life was too short to live in what had essentially become a platonic relationship. She filed for divorce and started to date. The first man she slept with was a revelation. " 'Oh my God,' I thought. 'I can't believe how good this is. I can't believe I gave this up for ten years!' I was just too idealistic in my twenties. You know, you think that love will conquer everything. But it doesn't. I'm telling you this painful personal story so that you can tell other people. Not everyone is good at sex. Kirby really tried, but he just didn't have any skill and it just wasn't something he ever felt comfortable with. I thought he could change at least enough to please me, but it just didn't work out. So don't expect everyone to be a good lover. And I guess I would have to say, 'Don't settle for someone without any talent.' "

Sex is important. A great sex life alone won't keep a couple together, but it sure helps. And a bad sexual relationship will leave one or both partners feeling frustrated, alienated, and even angry because they feel they are being deprived of sexual fulfillment in a society that heavily promotes the joys of sex. But talent in bed, like talent in tennis, is not universally distributed. Elaine spent ten years learning this lesson. Read it here, believe it, and get the lesson in ten minutes. Sex is a "talent" and while some people do learn it, for most it's like dancing or singing— experience, lessons, and motivation can make people better but won't make them gifted. There has to be raw talent to work with.

Here are some arguments people make in support of this myth:

There are a lot more important things in a relationship. Even if I am disappointed, bad sex won't affect our love or our commitment

Sex is not trivial. Our sexual attraction and our ability to give each other physical pleasure is a major facilitator and a creator of love and commitment. Our sexuality makes us more open and emotionally vulnerable. We expose our imperfect bodies and trust someone to make us feel whole and beautiful. During passion, we grit teeth, scream, make faces, or, in various ways, let down the relatively controlled and composed presentation of our self we give to the rest of the world. Some people may be able to have sex with anyone they find attractive, but most people can only function with someone whom they care about and who cares for them. Even people who are capable of recreational sex, and enjoy it, usually find sex with someone they love much more gratifying. In a great sexual relationship, partners feel grateful for the intense pleasure they can give each other and often, at heightened moments, looking into each other's eyes, feel almost compelled to say, "I love you." Couples who plumb the depths of each other's fantasies and sexual needs feel almost organically linked to each other. They feel they know each other's most private, essential self.

This is primal stuff. Sexual compatibility is very important in marriage—and it is a terrible loss if a couple stops sexually relating to each other. Yes, I know couples for whom illness or an accident has hampered or canceled out their sex life and who have adjusted and are still faithful and happy to be together, but it is still a huge compromise. And of course, this is under conditions beyond the partner's control—which makes a whole lot of difference. Sad to say, I do, however, also know couples for whom the disabling factor was a matter of bad luck, and even so, the other partner could not live with the fact that sexual activity had to be constrained. Sexual desire is a powerful emotion all by itself and, for most people, it is attached to their heart. While many marriages can and have withstood the diminution of a sex life or the deprivation of a sex life that never really got started, there is no doubt that this leaves a gap in the couple's relationship that destabilizes their commitment to each other.

Practice makes perfect. We'll get better. And if we don't, there is a whole field of sex therapy. We can learn if we get the right help

I could practice being a concert pianist from now until doomsday, and I would still get booed off the stage. Sometimes practice doesn't help—or it helps, but it just doesn't get you where you want to go. Maybe being a good lover seems easier than being an accomplished musician—but I'm not so sure. In a national study that sociologist Andrew Greeley interpreted, less than a third of those who responded thought their spouse was "a skilled lover." And some of those people were probably either ignorant or generous. It's not that "natural" to be talented in bed, and if you are starting out with someone who is so awkward that the experience isn't even minimally pleasing, then I wouldn't bet good money that just doing it a lot is going to make love-making fabulous.

Sex therapists can help. Therapists are really good at helping a man get over premature ejaculation or erectile failure. They can come up with some easy and good suggestions about how to cure problems like vaginal pain or dryness and they can, with counseling, reduce the anger that has accumulated between two people and interfered with working on the relationship and the desire to have sex together. A therapist can be an objective third party who focuses on the problem to be solved rather than on a person to be blamed. In other words, there are a lot of things therapists are good at, and they are certainly worth seeing.

But some problems have less of a guarantee. If someone has low sexual desire, that person is unlikely to become a passionate sexpot—at least in the present relationship. Low sexual desire is notoriously hard to "cure," although if it is a result of poor body image (a quite common cause), sexual trauma (such as childhood molestation), or impotence the prognosis is hopeful.

Some people, however, just aren't too interested in sex—and others aren't particularly good at following directions. Some people try and try to learn to ice-skate, but they can never just get up on their skates and glide away—or they get up, but just barely. Believe me, some people are the same about sex, and no amount of counseling is going to turn them into virtuoso sexual performers.

Can some partners turn into stars? Of course (especially if you catch them in early adulthood before they have learned a lifetime of bad habits). But don't bet on it. Even if you've got the best therapist in the world and even if you both are motivated to save the relationship, not everyone can be great at this. Adequate? Yes. Good? Probably. Outstanding? Unlikely.

Sex isn't that important— especially as you get older

Oh, yeah? Maybe if you are twenty-five, you think that at fifty, life is just going to be so mellowed out that you won't be looking for those same kinds of sexual highs that you enjoyed at twenty-one. Before you believe that, though, go ask a few of your older friends if they have a great sex life with their partner and be sure you ask honest ones. If they say their sex life is less than optimal, ask them if it bothers them. Some will say it's no big deal, but more than you might imagine will say it bothers them a lot—and a few might even be having affairs. Fifty or sixty seems impossibly old when you are twenty-five but, as all the sixty year olds who are reading this know, you can be pretty randy even if you are bald, fat, and half blind.

Think about all those years *before* middle age. Think you can forget about sex in your thirties and forties? Not too many people can. But let's say that you are one of those people who really doesn't need much sexual interaction and even when it's good, you can take it or leave it. Well, that may be okay for you, but can you guarantee that you will have a partner who will feel the same way? Even if neither of you organizes the meaning of life around sexual intimacy, that doesn't mean it won't turn into a big problem. Sex is like anything else: not so critical when it's fine and awfully important if it's awful.

Once my partner is relaxed with me, she will be able to be wilder. Gradually, the repertoire of what we can do will widen

Some partners just need confidence, trust, and a little experience—and they will try anything. It happens. But your best bet for a wild sex partner is the person who takes you apart the first time you have sex together. For most people, sex early on in a relationship is about as passionate as it gets. Granted, it takes time and trust to even think of, much less try, esoteric positions; it is common to have some inhibitions until you are sure of each other. Most people do not use trapezes early on in the relationship. Still, the desire for experimentation, for losing control is usually there in the beginning, if it's going to be there at all.

In fact, there is a scarier risk. Sometimes that passionate ability is *only there in the beginning, and once there is a commitment—poof! It's gone and all your partner wants is the missionary position once a month.* Now that's really not fair, but it happens, and not infrequently. There is no sure way to predict which Latin lover is going to turn into a siesta-loving couch potato (or which temptress will transform into a hausfrau). But if they start out uninterested in playful and experimental sex, your chances of getting it later are really slim.

But if my partner doesn't like certain acts, like oral sex, I can live without it

Does oral sex really matter? Say your beloved really likes intercourse and almost any position is open for negotiation. But he draws the line at oral sex. Is that the end of the world? Could be. Because suddenly, that's all you want. You loved it before, and now you can't get it. Now that bugs you! You feel deprived. You think *everyone* around you is having oral sex.

You get angry when you think about it. And you just know that the person who is flirting with you at work would be delighted to accommodate you. Will you be stalwart and just resign yourself to the situation? Or, if you are the person who doesn't want to perform a specific act, are you sure your partner can accept it without any compensatory activities? It's not clear how good anyone is at deprivation when restoration of the longed-for activity is only a proposition away.

So what should you do if the sex isn't good?

Don't get married. Or at least see if you can get help before you make a commitment

Well, the best answer is a good defense up-front—if you are dating someone now or living with someone and the sex isn't good, either get out while the getting is good or, if you are deeply in love, go to a sex therapist before you go any further and see what you can do about the situation. If your partner won't go, it will tell you a lot about what the future will be like. If your partner is willing to try, see where you can get to together, and with hope, it will be far enough. But remember, if the problem is low sexual desire, the long-term prognosis isn't good.

Stop faking

Chances are if you are already married or in a long-term relationship and things aren't great, you've been faking your response. You've been moaning and groaning, hoping that this would please your partner and perhaps turning up the heat so that things would be more passionate. If your partner hasn't figured out how to bring you to orgasm, you may be winning nightly Oscars for your rendition of a climax but not getting the pleasure you deserve (and if you are a guy and you are faking rock-hard erections, I am really impressed). Still your performance, even though it could get you a job in the porno industry, doesn't help fix anything in your relationship. On the contrary: you have been giving your partner inaccurate information, and he will never get any better unless he finds out how you really work. Imagine if you were teaching someone a language and you told him that everything he said was correct, even if it wasn't. It would be impossible for him to communicate with you or anyone else. If your partner continues to be a lousy lover, you helped make this miserable situation.

So, cut it out! One day when you are not in bed, fess up. You can pretty it up a little (too much truth could wilt your lover forever), but tell the essential facts as they are. You are not having orgasms, or it's too rough or too fast, or you need oral sex, or whatever it really is. Make sure it is all said in the context of a joint project: What would he like from *you* to make things more exciting? This is an excellent time to be vulnerable. Admit you have been too shy or too worried about his reaction to tell the truth before now—but you are biting the bullet and you know this will make for a better future. If this sounds too painful, then just say you'd like to try new ways of making love: for some reason the old ones just aren't working as well anymore. This will get you somewhere, but it's a second-choice strategy because it might not get you the same kind of motivation and commitment to a totally revamped sex life if that is what you really want.

Experiment

Sometimes you don't need a therapist or truth serum. What you need is to go to a romantic hideway, dim the lights, light some candles, drink champagne, and try out some sex toys and some outrageous X-rated videos. In other words, lose control, reinvent yourself or your partner when you both are comfortable enough and seduced enough not to care. The point is to get sexy and take a few risks. Even if the alcohol interferes with a peak performance, the important thing is to lose control and show each other that you are capable of romance—and even ecstasy. There are a lot of books, videos, and CDs that can help you figure out how to create the right mood and give you some new tricks to try (small personal suggestion: *The Great Sex Weekend,* a book I wrote a few years ago with Janet Lever). This tactic might give you some breakthrough experiences that would help introduce creativity and passion into the relationship. It certainly will help couples that are already doing well with one another but have just put sex on the back burner for too long a time. If things are more serious than that, go see a therapist—but whatever you do, don't wait for a bad sex life to get better all by itself. You could still be waiting while your partner has packed, left, and sent you a postcard from her new home in Fiji.

A note: If you're worried that it's you who isn't good in bed

If reading this has sent you into spasms of insecurity, I apologize: First because I hate to make anyone feel bad and, second, because you are probably a better lover than you think you are. The basics of being a great lover are to truly enjoy what you are doing, lose as many inhibitions as you can, be interested in almost anything, and be an acute observer and eager student of what makes your partner ecstatic. If you really want to be an unusually good lover, you will assume that you can always learn something new and that there are always new layers of your own and your partner's psyche to explore. There are books to read, couples seminars to go to, and new toys to try out. Treat sex as a wonderful adventure and take turns with your partner being the guide. Probably neither one of you is a virtuoso and, you know, that's just fine. As long as you make love well enough to please each other, you will be fine.

11

MYTH:
Masturbation by a partner in a relationship is a bad sign

Many, maybe most, traditional religions forbid masturbation. Why? Because most societies are procreation factories: all sexual urges should be channeled into intercourse. More intercourse increases the chances of more children. Until recently, societies were not worried about overpopulation; they were concerned about creating new bodies to till the ground, fill the factories, and die on the battlefields.

Much of current religious teaching reflects this concern for reproduction, and Judeo-Christian texts, among others, forbid wasting "seed" through "self-abuse." Even in societies where modern sex educators and contemporary cultural practices have made this taboo less powerful, a certain stigma remains. Touching oneself is seen as either immature and selfish, or shameful. Pleasure is only valid if it is produced for some utilitarian purpose: forming an emotional bond or creating a child. Many otherwise hip and liberated individuals feel that once they have a steady sexual partner, masturbation is just not allowable (much less desirable!).

I am not sure why this feeling still permeates the psyche of people who are liberated from religious dogma, but whatever the reason, it is time to get over it! Masturbation is one of the most natural (and efficient) ways an individual has for easing tension, ending frustration, and achieving sexual satisfaction. It doesn't cease to be natural or appropriate just because two people are married, living together, or dating. Masturbation is a totally different method of sexual pleasure than intercourse and is almost never a reflection of whether or not a couple has a good sexual relationship. On the contrary, any couple worth its sexual salt has numerous ways of enjoying their own and each other's body—and the likelihood is that the couple who celebrates each other's masturbation is a couple that has one hell of a dynamite sex life.

Here are some of the myths that get in the way.

If my partner loved me, there wouldn't be the need for masturbation

Masturbation usually has nothing to do with how much love there is in a relationship. Of course, there might be a correlation with a lack of affection if one partner is denying the other sexual access, or if the two partners are emotionally estranged. But most of the time masturbation is just another way of solving old-fashioned, physiological horniness. Look at it this way: The better sex is, the more someone wants. In other words, the better your sex life, the more sexually turned-on you and your partner are likely to be. What that means is that when you have an orgasm, it builds the need for more (after a suitable pause, of course). The less sex a person has, the less urgent the desire for more sex. I know this is counterintuitive, but it's true. So, actually, masturbating is often likely to occur in a relationship that is not only sexually adequate—but sexually superlative. The additional sexual need has nothing to do with love, but rather with increased appetite.

Masturbating really has nothing to do with how much attachment there is in most relationships. If this helps, put a new spin on the issue and think of food. When you eat a steak, it doesn't mean you don't like chicken. You could love *both* steak and chicken. And you wouldn't necessarily only want chicken when steak wasn't available. Some nights you would just feel like chicken, and it wouldn't make you love steak any less. Get it?

If our sex life was good enough, my partner would never want sex alone

Your sex life might be miraculous, the best sex life on the face of the planet, and still, your partner might want some time alone with her hand or a vibrator. Even if you use masturbation in your sex play together, there are times when someone wants to have sex all alone—free to indulge in private fantasies or some sex play that she might find inhibiting in the presence of another person. This doesn't mean your sex life together has a flaw; it just means there are some times when a person wants a private sexual moment.

Sometimes people don't want to make love—they just want to have an orgasm. Making love would take too much time. For example, Judy always experienced sexual tension when she was studying for exams. She could barely think until she had an orgasm. But the last thing she wanted to do was interrupt her studies for a long time. She was living with Auggie, who would have been more than happy to have obliged her. She says, "That would have been a big production. There would be foreplay, greasing up, and talk afterwards, and frankly I don't have time for that. I can get down on the floor, touch myself or use a vibrator and get off in a few minutes. Then I can get back to work. I really don't have the time or inclination to make love then. Auggie understands and when I close my study door, he respects that."

Masturbation is infantile. Intercourse is a mature form of sexuality

Let's get rid of this hierarchy thing. Both masturbation and intercourse are just fine. Sure, if everyone preferred masturbation so much that they quit having intercourse, the species would be in trouble. But rest assured this is not going to happen. What is true is that there is no such thing as one act being more mature or less mature than the other. We do start masturbation before we have intercourse—some infants are observed in their cribs rubbing against the sheets and enjoying the sensation. But early sexuality doesn't mean immature sexuality; it's just part of the training our bodies get about learning how to feel good.

If a man or woman places masturbation—either alone or as a couple activity—squarely in the center of his or her adult sexual life, it's perfectly mature. The point is not how you get pleasure, but that you create sexual pleasure in your relationship and learn how to give your partner what he or she needs and wants. As long as no one is hurt, there are no rules about what should happen in bed. I have heard women say that they feel degraded if their partner masturbates. But that is a product of how *they* feel about sexuality. It is not a fact, not a shared reality. Why not feel that your partner is sharing his or her innermost needs and fantasies in front of you and inviting you to be part of the turn-on? Or as Cecile says, "My lover likes to watch me touch myself. It is a turn-on for both of us. I can't really have an orgasm during intercourse, even though I enjoy it and enjoy my partner's excitement. But that's no big deal. We have our orgasms separately, and we have the presence of mind to watch each other—and get excited all over again. All this is making love. I don't know why people make distinctions about what order you do things in—or, for that matter, what you do!"

Masturbation is alienated sex—it avoids intimacy

As I've indicated, I don't think that masturbation necessarily has anything to do with less love, or less intimacy. On the other hand, I have also indicated that sometimes people use masturbation when they don't want intimacy—and that is fine, as long as they are getting intimacy at other times. And anyhow, why does sex always have to be intimate? We can have dinner and not insist that it always have to be romantic. Sometimes dinner is just functional and, sometimes, so is sex. Staying with food analogies (my second-favorite appetite), you could even imagine that you wouldn't want to have a five-course dinner every night, even if you could. Sometimes you just want to grab a sandwich on the fly. You don't have any negative feelings about the sandwich—you just want to gulp it down. If someone told you that was immoral, you'd laugh. It might be a disservice to the full range of culinary possibilities you could enjoy if you were always having a specially prepared gourmet meal, but you just don't have the time or desire to make a big deal out of every meal. The issue is not what you eat at any one moment in time, but the balance of *how* you eat over time.

And so it is with sex. Masturbation is convenient, but it won't cancel out the need for intimate and imaginative sexual interaction with another person. It will not be a fixation, and it will not alienate partners unless there is something drastically wrong with the relationship. Quite the contrary! In fact, given how hard it is for some partners to allow themselves to be watched during arousal or during orgasm, I'd argue that sometimes masturbation is extremely intimate, maybe even more intimate than intercourse. Letting a partner see how you arouse yourself is an emotionally vulnerable act. And also, for most people, a very sexy one. How much more intimate does it get?

Masturbation is a pale imitation of intercourse.
Why would anyone ever want second best,
when the best was available?

Did I say something about hierarchy? Can't we get away from the best and the worst? And anyhow, truth be told, it's not clear what is "best." After all, who knows your body best, you or someone else? The fact is that lots of men and women have told me that while they enjoy making love to their partner, when they get close to orgasm, they really want to apply the last strokes themselves because only they can do it exactly the way they need to in order to have the best possible orgasm. Philip, a twenty-five-year-old vice-president of a start-up software company talked frankly with me about the sexual adjustments he and his girlfriend of two years had had to make. "It took Alice awhile to accept the fact that no matter how great our sex life is together, I want to have my orgasm using my own hand. In the beginning, she would be going down on me or touching me and it would be great, but then she would get insulted when I couldn't come this way and I would want to finish myself. She would take my hand away and try to do it for me. But she doesn't do it hard enough or at exactly the right speed and it just gets frustrating and sometimes I can't have an orgasm at all if we try it that way too long. She would get all bent out of shape because she felt left out, but I explained to her that I have been masturbating a certain way since I was seven years old, so I'm like this finely tuned machine that has to be handled a certain way. Nobody who isn't inside of my skin can automatically know exactly what I need. It isn't because I don't love her enough, or because there is some other woman who could do it better than she. It's just the way I do it. Over time, she has understood and so now she has gotten into kissing and caressing me during these last few seconds, and that makes it even better for me. I think she gets turned on a lot by it, too."

Masturbation with a vibrator will become addictive, and satisfaction will become too difficult during ordinary intercourse

It is true that some women have a love affair with their vibrators. The vibrator gives an intensity of stimulation that is different—and perhaps more efficient—than any other kind of sexual sensation. But that doesn't mean women who love their vibrators don't want to be touched, or have oral sex, or intercourse. While it's true that some kinds of habituation can occur (for example, see Philip's discussion above), it is really the rare woman who, if she was ever able to have an orgasm during intercourse, loses that capacity. If she is impatient and doesn't want to wait for the slower buildup of sexual arousal during intercourse, she may want to reach for her vibrator. But the problem is not that she can't have an orgasm during intercourse or that she can't have a good time during intercourse but rather that she may have become a little too goal-oriented. The problem, then, isn't the vibrator; it's focusing on the end result. What's important is guaranteeing that sex with another person is collaborative and each person feels included and emotionally touched. If a partner feels displaced by a vibrator, then the couple should go back to the idea of sex as making love rather than as just a way to relieve sexual tension.

Still, what if a woman does like to have an orgasm with a vibrator? Why not? The point of intercourse is not for men to demonstrate that they are sexual gods, but to give pleasure and demonstrate love and affection. If a couple is using sex to bond, believe me, a great orgasm is a very bonding thing, no matter how it's delivered. Some men are so stuck on the idea that they have to give their partner an orgasm during sex that sex becomes an endurance test for both of them—and longer is not always better. Some women feel like Veronica when she told me what was wrong with her sexual relationship with her ex-husband. "Richard was always trying to show what a good lover he was instead

♥ *119*

of listening to me and reacting to what I wanted. He would always try to give me more than one orgasm, even if I didn't really want or need to have more than one orgasm. Sometimes I felt like he was treating me like a trained dog—proud of the tricks he could make my body do. Don't get me wrong. He was a very accomplished lover. But as time went on, there was just too much of him controlling me for me to enjoy it. He was really insulted that I even had a vibrator, or that occasionally I liked to touch myself to orgasm. He would take my hand away. He would make me promise not to use a vibrator while he was traveling. It made me lose respect for him. I couldn't respect someone that insecure."

Women's hesitations

Of course, there are also women who object to vibrators when their boyfriends or husbands suggest one. Some women think that if they can't have an orgasm during intercourse, another method indicates some kind of personal failure. They may feel that vibrators are too mechanistic or even feel guilty because orgasms with a vibrator are faster, more intense, and more predictable than trying to have an orgasm during intercourse. Some women won't even try a vibrator because they see them as antiromantic or unnatural.

What a mistake! It's like refusing to use a hair dryer because sunshine and air are a more natural process. The hair dryer is fast and sometimes produces a whole different, and better, result. Is there something dishonest about using a hair dryer? Come on! We'll use a lot more artifice than a hair dryer to have great-looking hair. So, then, following that logic, why wouldn't we use all the ways we can to have a great orgasm? Some women might add, yes we should, as long as it's not demeaning. But vibrators are not demeaning. Receiving pleasure and creating a sexual repertoire together can include anything you want, and it's not demeaning simply because it produces or precedes intercourse or uses batteries.

Masturbation is a good thing

It feels really dumb to have to state this conclusion—except that I know many of you really aren't sure masturbation *is* a good thing, But it is. It is a great part of a sexual experience—to use either alone or together. It will not threaten satisfaction with intercourse, and it may become a preferred way of having an orgasm—but so what? The pleasure you give yourself will not compete for a partner's love (so far, there is no recorded incidence of people proposing to their vibrators), and it can only add to the intimacy you feel for each other because you have found additional ways to create pleasure for each other. So here's a suggestion: Go as a couple to a sex shop. Or order a sex-toy catalogue and browse through it together. Pick out a couple of vibrators. (Why several? Different vibrators—internal, external, intense, light, etc.—produce different sensations.) Try them out together. Feel free to use them alone. Be happy, satisfied. Be pleased that you've given each other an erotic adventure. This kind of sexual exploration will not only create sexual satisfaction; it will also help create intimacy. Unless your relationship is troubled—and vibrators are part of your escape route—a masturbatory aid can be just one additional element in a closer, happier relationship. It is a myth, and a destructive one at that, to think that sexuality has to be partnered all the time, or always expressed through intercourse. Sexuality needs to be private some of the time, and playful a lot of the time. Get that down and you will have learned a lot about staying sexually alive and being a fulfilling sexual partner.

12

MYTH:
Women are not into sex toys, pornography, fantasy, or quickies

often talk with girlfriends about sex. We giggle about great sexual moments we have had in the past. Sooner or later, however,
some woman will utter a comment I have heard an uncountable
number of times: "I love my partner, but I'd give anything to have one
of those intense passionate moments again. I hate to think I'll never
have that kind of passion again. Our sex life is fine—but it's gotten routine. Most of the time I can take it or leave it. I hate feeling that way. I
fantasize about an anonymous night with a lover."

We have conflicting images of female sexuality: the temptress and
the faithful wife—the first, a no-holds-barred wildcat; the second, a
cow-eyed trusting model of femininity who must be made love to as
if she were made out of porcelain. But what I'm now going to tell
you is true for millions of women, if not for every single one: Women
are both temptress *and* wife and if men always treat sex as a sacred

and serious act, women are going to be bored silly. Believe me, if there is enough passion in the bedroom, women won't care where you touch them because the point won't be if they've had an orgasm or not that evening—the point will be ecstasy! And ecstasy isn't necessarily about an orgasm. It is about being so turned-on that you have not only transcended the moment, you have also transmogrified into some kind of beast, some kind of animal that is all instinct and desire—to the point where you are at the edge where pleasure and pain are indistinguishable and you are one mass of quivering eros.

David Schnarch writes in his book *The Crucible of Sex,* and its more popular version, *The Passionate Marriage,* that this kind of eros could be called "wall-socket sex." Hundreds of couples come to his seminars to try and find out how they can have a piece of that—or at least get back the old zing they used to have in their relationship. They spend a lot of money reconnecting and, from what I hear, they get their money's worth. But I'm going to give you what I think is the secret to unbelievable sex, and it will only cost you what you've already paid for this book: The essential element of the Schnarch program is that men and women stop performing for each other and learn how to enjoy their own pleasure. They stop being performance conscious and they go for what they need—each person being delighted to learn from the other person what his or her deepest desires and needs are and each person feeling free and confident to get what he or she needs. Partners can look deeply into each other's eyes during sex because they are comfortable in themselves. They feel the deepest intimacy coming together as two individuals who are giving each other everything they need and want. Ah . . . But how do you get there? Well, I can't do Schnarch's seminar—you'll have to go there for that—but I can give you some information that will help you create, develop, or retrieve passion—but only if you stop making love all the time and start having sex.

Sex doesn't always have to be about love

Of course, sex will be more amazing if you are deeply in love—but love is usually erotic when the relationship is very young, and it is the charge of achieving love and the amazement at having it that still fires sexual life.

After a while what is required is penetration of the deeper psyche and the development of a sexual life that is neither generic nor programmed. I want to counter the central assumption that sex is always best when it's about making love and that the proof of success is the predictable production of orgasms. It's just not true to think that merely having an orgasmic partner is proof that you have a good sex life. And it's a myth to think that the "need" for gadgets, games, and fantasy means that something is wrong with the essential chemistry between partners. I assure you that orgasms are not the sine qua non of great sex. Even orgasms can get boring, not to mention the fact that most people can give themselves pretty great ones. What is necessary in order to be a great lover is the creation of sexual interest over a long time. And to do that, you have to throw away politically correct visions of sexuality and get down to what really works and what turns both partners on. Here are a couple of ideas about exploring eros and fending off boredom.

"Playing passion" creates passion

Every night can't be a passion festival. There is a place for sweet seduction, conversation, and gentle arousal. We all want romantic moments. But sometimes, a steady diet of that makes women long for the sexuality of fantasy—of gothic novels where the brooding master of the household can restrain himself no longer, and shows up in his lady love's bedroom unbidden and takes her. She gives token resistance of course, but this is, indeed, what she has truly longed for.

I know men are reading this and going, "Arrrghhh! What slop!" And they are also thinking that if they indulge that fantasy, they'll go to jail for rape or sexual harassment. (Keep that last thought in mind if you are just dating someone: This scenario only works in real life between two people who are keyed in to each other's fantasies and know that scenarios like this are acceptable and desirable to both of them.) But believe me, a large number of women (and not a few men!) want to be treated like the ripest fruit on the tree: taken, eaten, devoured—a testament to how irresistible they are, how deep the need their lover has for them.

There are scenes in movies that demonstrate the kind of pure passion that men and women want. There is a scene between Al Pacino and Ellen Barkin in *Sea of Love* that passion junkies know well. Pacino slams her against a wall (but not in a bad way) and they tear at each other like animals. Those few moments have given some women fantasy material for years.

Toys

Wake up, men, and embrace this concept! Toys are not your enemy, not the competition, but an ally, a friend, your comrade in arms! Many men look at vibrators as buzzing proof that they are not doing a good-enough job. They feel their six inches of flesh is displaced by this six ounces of plastic. Do you feel this way? If so, please, please, get over it. Women love vibrators—but they love them best when *you* are holding them, using them to get things heated up so that an orgasm during intercourse or anything else is assured. I know, some of you feel that once a woman likes using a vibrator a lot (a sure test is if you turn one on, she'll come bounding in out of the garden, salivating) a certain amount of sensitivity to touch gets lost in the process. But even if that were true (and I don't think it is), what do you care? The point is to give her mind-boggling pleasure with your hands, or using your feet, or whatever works. And even if she uses it a lot, think of it this way: Sometimes people eat between meals, but it doesn't mean they don't want to sit down to dinner!

Vibrators come in various shapes and sizes—some buzz, some don't. There are dildos to use with vibrators or separately. And don't forget blindfolds, handcuffs, little tiny whips that sting just enough to feel good. Any sex shop worth its salt has at least two shelves of things you probably haven't thought of, much less tried. Open up your eyes and bring these little gifts home instead of flowers . . . be playful, imaginative. Do this a couple of nights in a row and she'll be waiting at the door for you—and I'm not kidding. What you are trying to do is increase experimentation, trust, and sensation; and a long-term sexual relationship needs all of that. And don't forget—men get to try these things on for size as well. Don't let that little vibrator scare you. They are not just for women—as long as you don't get prudish and think of it as a "female thing." Gay guys, who are infinitely more imaginative lovers than most heterosexual men, know that playthings are good for their relationship and that they increase the arousal barometer a whole lot. Don't get squeamish. Even if you are fine with bread-and-butter sex, your partner might not be. And you may not have begun to find out what the two of you are capable of together.

Pornography

Most women say they don't like pornography—but there is research to indicate that might not be the case. In a recent study in which both men and women were given pornography to watch, a lot of the men, predictably, liked it, while most of the women, predictably, said they did not; this is the type of finding usually reported in the research literature. However, this particular study had an additional truth meter: both men and women were rigged up with a gadget called a plethysmograph, which measures blood flow. When blood moves into the genital area because of arousal, this is noted, and can give an accurate gauge of state of mind. Indeed, many of the women who indicated no interest in or some distaste toward the materials recorded a very significant state of physiological arousal. The researchers concluded that either the women were embarrassed about their interest in the pornographic movies and felt they ought to say they were uninterested in them or they were aroused but didn't know it. The latter is an interesting thought. Some women may have a strong disconnect from their bodies when the context of the situation isn't "right." If they think they are not supposed to be aroused, they may not code a body response as erotic. (Kind of like the question about the tree that falls in the forest with no one to hear it does it make a sound?)

But believe me, some women do hear the tree fall, and erotic movies are a great sexual hors d'oeuvre for many of them. Even though some of these movies are sexist and piggy to the max, enough heat can be generated to have a very good time. There are also, just as an aside, some women-made movies that are not denigrating to females, such as those made by Candida Royale (an unfortunate stage name, but a very nice and talented person). These flicks were made to be a turn-on instead of a turnoff to visually sensitive females who like explicit sexuality but can't tolerate the macho stuff the male hard-core industry churns out. There are other like-minded products if you are interested, and you can find them at Eve's Garden in New York, Good Vibrations in San Francisco and Berkeley, and on various websites such as Playboy.com, Condomsense.com, and Xandria.com. Why look? Because both women and men enjoy being on the erotic edge. Because games and gadgets are a turn-on—and when they aren't, they are at least worth a good laugh together, which is also a lot of fun.

Fantasy

Most books tell you fantasy is just a little addition to your sex life, something you might want to add to your sex play with your partner sometime. But fantasy is not an unimportant or small thing in a couple's sexual life together. Fantasy is more of a pathway to a deeper sexual connection than almost anything else you can do together. Most men and women have a secret sexual life that their partners (and even their psychiatrists) may never know about. They have fantasies old and dear that are at their erotic core—and many of them are pretty weird. That's why they don't share them. But if you can get into your partner's head and if you can get these fantasies shared and used as part of your erotic moments together, it is an extraordinary bonding experience. Fantasies are not necessarily what anyone wants to happen in real life, but they exist because they serve some core erotic function; they release part of the erotic imagination that nothing else quite touches. Sometimes they are merely reruns of great experiences, but other times they are the desire that was wished for, but unachieved, and this is the only way to make it real.

Some fantasies involve imagining potentially degrading experiences that are erotic. Even if the act couldn't be done in real life without disastrous results, it can remain supercharged for the person who uses this fantasy. Examples might include an orgy, sadomasochism, or even changing genders. The fantasies are so erotically powerful *because* they are so taboo, so sordid. They are profoundly private but share them together and you will have a kind of electricity that is at the magma level of erotic connection. Let me describe a guy who has all this down right.

Dillon looks like an ordinary midwestern clean-cut guy, which is certainly part of who he is. Head of his own company, father of one, good buddy to several friends, he is well liked in his community. He is respectful to women, and during most of his seventeen-year marriage he was monogamous and orthodox about his sexuality: It was mostly missionary position, a certain amount of oral sex, and nothing much out of the ordinary.

As the marriage started to fade, however, he started to look around, thinking he could keep the marriage going if he had an outside sexual life that kept him happy. He and his wife hardly made love anymore (she told him she didn't enjoy making love with him that much), his ego suffered and, of course, so did his desire. Part of his quest outside the marriage was to see if he really was a dud in bed or if he and his wife were just a bad match.

At first he was his usual good-natured, what-can-I-do-for-you self with the women he met, who were only too happy to go to bed with him, married or not. But he was amazed at how demanding, neurotic, and spoiled some of these women were. Since he wasn't in love and wasn't trying to be the dutiful husband, he tried taking on a new persona. He spoke roughly, dominated them in bed—and they loved it and became compliant.

Dillon perfected this technique to a science. He would romance a woman, then when in bed, probe her deepest fantasies, watch her reactions, and find out that most of the time they dealt with being sexually dominated and, at the core, sexually voracious. He was a big success with a lot of women who meant nothing to him.

When he finally left his wife, he discovered that he was, as he put it, "meant to be married." His whole emotional being was monogamous, even if he hadn't been acting that way. On a business trip, he met a woman who was his equivalent in his industry, and they hit it off right away. He was hesitant, though, about using his newfound approach in bed, but he did. And it worked like a charm. But because he liked this woman so much and because she became more special to him, after they had been going out a long time, he backed off on his fantasy dialogue and toys during lovemaking. He was afraid the toys and sex games that he had become accustomed to and were so erotic to him would make her feel cheap or unloved.

He was surprised, but delighted, when she asked him not to stop. "I guess I thought all those games were a little too much for a love relationship, but I think I was carrying around some old stereotypes. We not only kept using toys, but our sex life got wilder and wilder—we are both exhibitionists, and we got into that in a big way. After a time we both unveiled some pretty heavy fantasy materials including some of mine that I had never told anyone, not my wife, not my best friend, no one. We have tried to bring some of the safer ones to life and we play psychologically with the others. It is very hot, very intimate. I am more in love with her because of it and I am pretty sure she is more in love with me because of it, too."

Moral: Don't be timid. Men, don't think of her as Snow White, and don't be Prince Charming. Women, don't *be* Snow White if you want excitement. Find something real, forbidden, and unique to the two of you. Have a sex life that is forged between you and not something that is generically predictable that could automatically get the Good Housekeeping Sexual Seal of Approval. This is your private life, and you can make it just as hot as you want it to be. One of the greatest advantages of a trusting, safe, and loving relationship is that you can try things and know your partner will not let you down. Now that's love and commitment!

13

MYTH:
Men are simply not monogamous by nature; women are

There are the endless movie scenes: the randy guy walks from his girlfriend's house to his *other* girlfriend's house. The wife reaches into her husband's pocket and finds a love note from another woman. On and on, men are shits and women have hormones that hit only for one man. If a woman is a free spirit in the movies, she is usually about to get wiped out, either right then, or at the end of the film. She is too wild to survive.

And there is a lot of science (much of which is pseudoscience) telling everyone that men and women just can't help being what they are. Sociobiology and psychobiology have come along with what has become a mantra: the selfish gene. Men want to impregnate as many women as they can (or at least that's where the faithless urge comes from) to pass on their DNA; and women, having the possibility for fewer offspring, have to invest in quality not quantity and therefore choose their bed partners very carefully. It all makes sense, except that if you look really carefully, this stereotyping doesn't fit the data. And what data it does fit have a pretty good cultural explanation: In most societies if a woman is openly nonmonogamous she gets killed or something else really nasty happens to her. But with all that, do women really not want any nonmonogamous contact? Do they want just *one* guy?

Not in the animal world. There are some wonderful studies about faithless female robins who left their guy guarding the nest, feeding the children, while scientists who analyzed the fledglings' DNA find that a good 50 percent of the babies were the product of another daddy. Likewise, anthropologist Helen Fisher, analyzing exhaustive ethnographic files, has found that women in tribal societies change partners more often than the sociobiologists would have us believe and a lot of it is timed to when the last child stops breast-feeding and the mother is fertile again. Then quite a few mothers are out in the sexual marketplace looking for the next, better father, and some of them start looking for the new Dad before the old one has gone away. Fisher finds plenty of societies where women keep a few men on a string in order to get what they need out of each one of them.

So how did we get trapped with all this Mars and Venus imagery—where men roam and women want to stay home? Let's investigate some common exaggerations.

Men are more sexual by nature

If by "sexual" you mean they masturbate a lot, and more, than women, I'll buy that. Or if you would substitute number of fantasies, I grant you that as well. Or I will even say that men might like a higher rate of intercourse with their partners than women do, although not significantly higher, and I'm not sure that rate remains stable in long-term marriage when a lot of women complain that their husbands are more likely to claim a headache than they are. But I will grant you that most men want to have intercourse sooner after childbirth than women do (now there's a shocker!). And perhaps they have more sexual desire under iffy situations (they had a fight—he's still interested, she can't believe it!).

Still, these differences hardly put men into a different sexual class than women—and differences in masturbation, fantasy, or desire for an extra sexual round each week do not predict infidelity. All of this is a far cry from nonmonogamy. The facts support me. Sociological research shows that relatively few men *or* women believe in nonmonogamy (about 10 to 15 percent). While cheating on your wife, husband, girlfriend, or boyfriend happens, it is the rare person who makes a hobby of it, the rare person who feels no guilt at all. Men included.

But if you look at the newest nonmonogamy statistics drawn from a large scientific survey (a National Opinion Research study reported in the *The Social Organization of Sex,* University of Chicago Press, 1998), you can see that this standard of fidelity is breaking down a bit. There is more nonmonogamy by far among *both* men and women if they are under twenty-five. So the standard (or maybe just personal discipline) might be changing. On the other hand, you should know that the statistics for young men and young women are very similar, supporting my contention that when the penalties for nonmonogamy start to be equal, the behavior starts to be more equal too.

Even if men aren't wildly nonmonogamous, they are only held down by being with a woman

I think there is something to this. Gay men are the sexual athletes of the world. But they had a lot more sex outside of their relationships when there were no consequences. Once AIDS came along the gay culture modified and what was considered moral behavior changed pretty damn quick. Partner protection became paramount. Keeping a good healthy partner upped the ante in terms of whether or not to go outside the relationship for sex. Gay magazines started touting the joys of monogamy. Sound familiar? As gay guys started to have incentives for being faithful, more became just like heterosexual men.

But imagine if women and men had the same sexual freedom to-gether that same-sex male couples still do: no chance of pregnancy, no angling for marriage. And as long as we are fantasizing, let's imagine a sexual world where there were no sexually transmitted diseases that would threaten our lives or our fertility. Now add to this new sexual uni-verse an absence of any sexual double standard whatsoever. Don't you think that might change the description of men's and women's sex lives?

And as long as we've put in same-sex couples as an example, let's take a good look at lesbians. While they espouse monogamy more than gay men, psychological and sociological research shows that they practice it a heck of a lot less than heterosexual women (see Philip Blumstein and Pepper Schwartz, *American Couples: Money, Work, and Sex,* William Morrow, 1983, or the work of researchers Anne Peplau and Larry Kurdek). Without the constraints and scripts of marriage, there is a lot more bouncing from bed to bed than heterosexual life prescribes. It may not be the same as among gay men—but it does indicate there is a lot more room on the continuum of monogamy for women than we thought there was.

Men are more sexually aggressive. They see something they want, and they just go after it. Women are more circumspect and therefore do less

Well this makes no sense at all. If men were so forceful, so aggressive, wouldn't a lot more women be having sex outside of marriage too? Or do these men only pick on single women? And anyhow, I'm not so sure I go along with the idea of the forceful male. Go to a party and what do you see? One brave guy and ninety-nine chickens of both sexes. In fact, in some cases I would say women are by far the more predatory creature.

Ask most good-looking men if they have ever been propositioned by a married woman. I think you will find it a common experience—and a lot of these men were shocked. Women often assume that men are up for any even moderately attractive woman and are hurt and embarrassed when they are refused. But a lot more men believe in their vows than we think and find themselves the target more often than they are the archer.

Women need love; men just need opportunity

Let me reiterate the above point. There are plenty of women, just as there are a good many men, who think that casual sex would be just fine. Just for fun (I won't call this science), I asked eight young men at a local grocery store if a woman had ever wanted them to deliver more than their groceries. Four of these boys said yes, and two said they had complied, one with a sixty-five-year-old woman (who, this gallant lad remarked, was really well put together and a great experience). In the classic film *The Graduate,* Mrs. Robinson is seen as a lustful and immoral woman—perhaps in the same way we would regard a man who tried to seduce the adult girlfriends of his son or the college-age daughters of his friends. Perhaps this was the first portrayal in a major contemporary film of the mother of a twenty year old as a horny, sexy woman. Whatever their place in history at the time, we know now that predatory Mrs. Robinsons exist just as we know that predatory Mr. Robinsons do.

Every man might not be nonmonogamous, but every man would like to be

I really think this is an unjust rap. There are a lot of family men out there just as there are a lot of women who never ever even think about straying. A woman I know, a sexual adventuress, once thought it would be fun to give her husband what every man is supposed to fantasize about: a three way. She suggested it as a present for their fifteenth wedding anniversary and said he just about "lost his cookies." "He thought I needed counseling. He thought I was obscene. We had sort of a fight about it because I thought he was being so much of a prude I couldn't believe it. It wasn't just that he didn't want to do it—he thought I was cracked to even imagine he would."

Remember that a large part of American society, and the world, is religious and people take their religion's sexual guidelines very seriously. Nonmonogamy might be an exciting thought to the less observant, but to the hundreds of thousands of men who take their Bible or other holy book seriously, nonmonogamy is a sin against God. Even the thought is uncomfortable. So whatever the stereotype, don't assume that all men harbor the secret desire to cheat. As Eddie, who used to be a very successful stage actor, put it, "My family and I are very close. We are extremely honest. We read scripture almost every night and God is a presence in our household. I think some people think that makes us conservative in all ways. It doesn't. I used to be in show business; I know what can go on. But that is not who I am, and I think my life and my marriage are richer because of our trust and the integrity of our vows. Because I have been in the spotlight, I know there are women who do not respect that I take my vows seriously. I have had to have some uncomfortable conversations both when I was on stage and even now, as a surgeon. But it isn't hard for me; it's hard for them. I know what is meaningful to me. It is my contract with my wife and with God."

Okay, so women have sex outside of marriage, but it's only the glamorous "new women." They are exceptions and are unlike other women

Excuse me, but female nonmonogamy is as old and as common as male nonmonogamy; otherwise, there wouldn't be so many rules and regulations and awful punishments (remember stoning to death?). And for these reasons, we don't find out about it as much. Let me tell you a story a friend of mine told me about his brother, and I've heard others like it. My friend was the son of a very religious, very traditional mother. He was one of eight children, each of whom felt that their mother had existed purely for him or her. When he was sixty, he attended a reunion of all the siblings—something that hadn't happened for a very long time. Each of them told a story about their sainted mother, and what emerged was that each of them remembered at some point walking in on her in some kind of affectionate embrace with Casey, their good neighbor and friend from a nearby farm. One by one the stories multiplied, until it got to the youngest brother, who, it could not be avoided noticing at this point, looked different from the rest of them and was, yes, the spitting image of Casey. It was at that moment, and not before, that their mother's secret life and the secret of their youngest brother were known to each of them, including the youngest. This is a woman who would not have turned up on any sex surveys, and it is unlikely her husband ever knew that anything was amiss in their household.

The exceptions who everyone thinks are the rule

Of course there are nonmonogamous types, people who cannot resist the call of the wild. But these people exist among *both* men and women. Allow me to list a few types that have a bit more chance than usual of spreading themselves around: the powerful, the insecure, the romantic, and the too beautiful.

The powerful
Why are powerful people more likely to be nonmonogamous? Because they get asked more (can you imagine how many times some-

one like Michael Jordan got asked?) and they get refused less ("Uh, gee, Mr. President, I just *couldn't* . . ."). Granted, more men than women are powerful, hence higher body counts for men than for women. But if we could survey comparably famous and successful women, there would probably be a higher number than among most other groups of women.

The insecure

Some people need more than one person to feel lovable or sexy or whatever. For some reason, they cannot convince themselves they are desirable even with repeated success. They are reassured only for the moment, then need a new compliment. Sometimes men and women outgrow this trait—but not always. This kind of person cannot resist the conquest and the brief but satisfying ratification it brings with it. This seems to be more common among men than women, perhaps because sometimes men who were unhappy about the way they looked and interacted with women when they were younger often gain cachet when they get successful and want to make up for all the things they thought they missed. As we mentioned above, fewer women get the chance to have this change in status. It may also be that women stop sooner because of children and the higher cost associated with being found out if you are playing around with too many random bodies. Or it may be that women grow up sooner. Some people think so.

The romantic

There are some men and women in love with love. They may not have many affairs, but they cannot resist a relationship that seems like an affair of the heart. This often is the saga of the multiply married—the men and women who get married three or four times only leaving one marriage when their heart is "taken away" by the newest love. I have met men who just find women wonderful and don't want to miss any of them. A lot of these men love love and are a lot less fond of everyday life. They love beginnings, and who can blame them—except their wives. It is interesting to ponder, however, why the newest woman thinks that she will truly be treated differently than the others. All the rest of this guy's marriages began the same way, but obviously hope springs eternal and women feel that they are the true anointed destiny. But I shouldn't make this sound just like a male pattern. Falling in and out of love and in and out of bed because of it is a common theme for lesbians, who have the additional hazard of having good friends who can turn into lovers if the timing is right. Love, being venerated by women, creates a context in which sex is justified. I have heard from women many times in interviews that when they met their "soul mate," they could not turn away from the love affair.

The too beautiful

Beauty may be in the eye of the beholder—but some people seem to please a lot of beholders. While an absolutely beautiful person isn't guaranteed to be nonmonogamous, nonetheless, such people get used to being adored and it's hard to give it up. Models, athletes, and other famous and well-built people have more than their share of bodies in their past and sometimes in their present—love one at your own risk. But don't think your risk only applies if the beauty is a man—in most cases, the power of beauty creates its own destiny, and this affects both men and women similarly.

So what does this mean to you?

If you are a woman with a sexual appetite that gnaws at you even though you are married, at least you know you are not abnormal. If you are a guy who never has a thought of another woman but the one at home, at least you know you are not so unusual. If you are committed to someone or married to her or him, this new vantage point I am giving should warn you not to take your partner for granted and assume that your relationship's monogamy is guaranteed just because you said it was during the ceremony and your initial discussions with each other. It never helps to have blinders on in life or to believe the myths that get handed down about male and female sexuality—even if the same myths get passed around by a lot of people. As I said earlier, non-monogamy, or the capacity for it, is part of a species trait—and culturally variable depending on the costs and benefits at any one point in time. So now that you know that, file it away for when you need it.

14

MYTH:
You can't have really great
sex without intercourse

Actually, I would consider the idea that you can't have really great sex *with* intercourse. Well, maybe that's a little too strong, but honestly, lovemaking is and should be about so much more than following some sort of script that sex has got to revolve around putting a penis into a vagina.

Most people think that if sex doesn't at least involve intercourse as the final triumphant ending to the lovemaking session, something essential has been missed. But if the truth be told, making intercourse predictable makes sex predictable, and *excellent sex* and *predictability* are words and concepts that do not really belong in the same sentence. Once sex starts to happen in a routine fashion, the possibilities for surprise, anticipation of surprise, experimental discovery, and over-the-top eroticism become much less likely. Oh sure, you don't see this happen when you first fall in love or lust; then even being hit by a two-by-four would feel swell. But once the relationship matures a bit and the edge is just a little bit rounded, it is easy for sex to become routine. Still, even people who hate the idea of "vanilla sex" still think that intercourse is sacrosanct. And it isn't just men who feel this way. Some well-done studies have indicated that, if anything, women feel more strongly about it than men! Talk about your false consciousness and great PR job! Whoever has been selling women the idea that intercourse is the best way to get sexual pleasure ought to get salesman of the millennium! As most men and women know, a huge number of women never have an orgasm during intercourse. If an orgasm is what they are looking for (and there is a fairly good chance that it is high on their personal agenda), they usually need additional stimulation by their partner's mouth, fingers, or a well-applied vibrator. Most women know this, and yet they want to make sure intercourse occurs sometime during a lovemaking session.

Why are we so fixated on this as the main event? Here are some reasons why I think we fixate on intercourse

It's "normal"

There is this weird idea that if you don't have intercourse every time you have sex, you are messed up. I'm not sure where this comes from. Maybe it's some vestige left over from the most conservative of sexual philosophies. The idea is that every time you have sex it has to have the possibility of resulting in pregnancy. Now I know there are still a few orthodox religions that believe every act of intercourse should have at least the chance of resulting in conception, but most modern men and women aren't buying that approach. (And my guess is that if you are reading this book, you aren't committed to an orthodox approach to sex either.) Most of the time when we make love we are hoping for just the opposite: We don't want a pregnancy. So, if we are trying not to get pregnant, what's the big deal about intercourse? Is it the only approved way of getting pleasure? Well, for some people, I suppose it is. We have these awful inheritances of guilt about sex anyhow. Or we think that we are not supposed to use our hands (that would be masturbating) or mouth (that would be gross) or a vibrator (that would be unnatural because it isn't a body part). We forget that our bodies were made for sensation—almost every part we have likes being touched, stroked, tweaked, and entered. We are a bundle of nerve endings, all of which get engaged if someone is an artful enough lover. There is nothing abnormal about using every part of the body for sex. If it feels good, it's probably good for us (with the possible exception of anal intercourse, which might need to be approached with caution and a rubber because of all those little microbes that love to live in anal tracts). And even here, it is clear that the anus was meant to be a sexy area. There are all kinds of nerve endings in the vicinity. And many men have orgasms when their prostate is stroked that make other kinds of orgasm feel ho-hum. So the bottom line (I can't resist these cheap jokes . . .) is that almost everything is fair game if we are at ease with the idea that, at least most of the time, sex is about pleasure any old way we can produce it. And any way we can produce pleasure is normal, because our bodies were made for it.

Sex wouldn't be complete without it

Who says? Granted, many of us wouldn't want to have a hot session of sex without an orgasm; but the most effective orgasms don't need to include intercourse. Many of you know that women usually need additional clitoral stimulation to have a climax, and almost all women will have an orgasm more quickly if they are touched before or during intercourse. But some of you may not know that there is a large number of men out there who like intercourse but come more quickly, and strongly with oral sex or during masturbation, or some combination of the two. A fabulous lovemaking session, it seems to me, is about a great orgasm at the end of an ecstatic buildup. If you are close to having an orgasm during oral sex, why switch to intercourse when it may break up what is a very satisfying set of sensations?

He needs it

"But," she says, "he needs it!" Does he really? Have you ever tried to engage in foreplay so artfully that he begs for more of the same? Actually, I think a lot of women go straight to intercourse not because he needs it, but because it's really a lot easier to do than giving oral sex or figuring out just how to make him come by touching him. Intercourse is sometimes the lazy woman's way of giving a man an orgasm. He would probably be just as happy being tantalized by touching and oral stimulation and teased until he just can't stand it anymore. But granted, that takes a little more effort.

She needs it

Well, she may think she does. A woman will try hard to be whatever it is her lover needs her to be, and he needs her to want him. So she shows how much she wants him, begging him to enter her. Pardon me for being a bit skeptical. I'm sure sometimes she just can't wait to be entered, but sometimes it just doesn't feel that necessary, yet she's still begging for it—if she thinks that's the validation he needs to get. Most of the time she might be able to take it or leave it, as long as she is being skillfully stimulated in some other way. There are a whole lot of women who have an orgasm by being touched or licked or who would love it if their partner started with that kind of foreplay and finished with it. I have heard this statement—and I apologize for forgetting who first penned it: "Foreplay is something that happens before your partner forgets about you." Women love those moments when lovemaking is not yet frenzied, not yet lost in one's own pleasure, but still sensual,

communicative, and building in excitement. The slower, even lan-
guorous, stroking of foreplay does not replace the pleasures of intercourse, but neither is it second best. If a woman remembers that it is
mutual pleasure the two partners are after, rather than the necessity of
having certain acts all the time, or a set order in which acts have to happen, she will let go of relying on just one sexual script and enjoy the
variety that each lovemaking session will bring.

If we don't have intercourse, my partner will think I am strange or withholding

It's true, many people are afraid to ask for something or do something different because they are insecure and don't want to be seen as
strange or manipulative. And to some extent, they are right. Women are
so convinced that all men need intercourse that if a guy wants to stay
away from it for a while and savor other options, his partner is likely to
think there is something wrong, feel rejected, or impute his actions to
some dark sexual hangup. If a woman wants to concentrate on other
ways to make love, her partner may think she is trying to punish him,
doesn't trust him, or is playing some kind of mind game with him. It is
hard to not think of intercourse as the ultimate act of lovemaking. Still,
if the couple talk about their commitment to sexual exploration and
invention, there shouldn't be any feeling that an evening of love that
omits intercourse is letting the other person down, or is a commentary
that something is wrong with the relationship.

I have trouble with foreplay

We criticize men for being selfish or women for not liking certain
acts, but I think some of people's dependence on intercourse has to do

with the fact that it feels more mutual to them. Both men and women often feel self-conscious about receiving pleasure. They worry that they are treating their partner callously, as if they were asking to be "serviced." Even when their partner tells them they like giving oral sex or touching them to orgasm, they still feel that they are being selfish. They want to stop foreplay so they can at least be doing the same thing to each other at the same time. But learning to accept pleasure and be the focus of attention is, in its own way, as much of a skill as learning how to give it. I am convinced we wouldn't race toward intercourse as quickly as we do if we could believe that the partner who is touching us is really happy making us happy.

Partners like to do what they think they do well. I can only surmise from the short time spent on most foreplay (at least among heterosexual couples; lesbians report spending a lot more time at it!) that people just don't feel competent at it. Intercourse seems to call for less finesse; banging away at each other in a frenzy masks the more demanding issue of how well you are pleasing your partner. Of course slow, probing intercourse could have the same feeling and pace as foreplay, but how many men have intercourse that way? Intercourse quickly becomes goal-directed for most couples. Sometimes women will even do what they can to make their partner come quickly, feeling a thrill of sexual power as they cause their lover to give in to his excitement. Intercourse becomes a predictable and easy way to be a good lover; being great at foreplay seems harder, so it is avoided.

How do you benefit from less intercourse?

But you might be saying to yourself: We are only choosing between great and greater—what's the big deal? *Why not* always include intercourse? Because then intercourse becomes the main event and everything else is just the warm-up act. Women feel they are being lubed up just for the moment when he begins to have pleasure instead of feeling that pleasure begins from the first flirtatious look. Men may resent the idea that a woman just does enough foreplay to get him hard enough to penetrate her. A man also wants to feel that a woman who is having oral sex with him or touching other parts of his body wants to be there and is not just doing this to get him excited enough to get erect. Plus, there are some additional benefits:

Long, luxurious, effective foreplay

There are orgasms and there are astounding orgasms. Why not build up to one so slowly and intensely that your whole body is aching? We know that women usually love this kind of slow body tune-up. A woman will be wildly turned on, and usually she will want to continue the same kind of stimulation that has gotten her so excited. If the whole program is petting and sucking or using various toys, she doesn't have to worry that just when everything feels perfect her partner is going to decide that this is the time to stop what is working so well— and start having intercourse. As good as that may feel, it may be just the wrong thing at that moment. She loses the momentum toward an orgasm, sex becomes somewhat more mechanical, and the feeling has to rebuild. If she knows that stimulation is going to keep going until she is satisfied—she can relax more—get into it and not worry that it's going to stop.

Men are the same way. A lot of men like to be touched in a certain way and in a certain rhythm. If their partner is giving them great oral sex, they may get into the pace of that stimulation and want it to continue in that exact way until orgasm. If their partner just stimulates them until they are close, they will, of course, love having the orgasm inside of her; but it is also true that some orgasms would be even more amazing because of the sheer eroticism of ejaculating in her mouth or hand—or in any unexpected way.

Orgasms that don't take so much work to get!

One of the nice things about taking intercourse off the menu now and then is that it is easier on the guy, especially if you normally make love in the missionary position. If a woman is slow to come, and many are, the thrusting can go on so long that it is a lot like work. Men's legs or calves cramp up, they start to sweat, muscles start to ache: not exactly what you'd like to feel at your highest and best moment. Let's face it, a lot of intercourse takes a certain amount of athleticism—and not all guys have it. Plus, most women have experienced intercourse that just goes on too long. Of course, usually the complaints are in the opposite direction, but too long can be as bad, or worse, than too short. Women get sore, even very sore, and the more uncomfortable it is, the dryer and more out of the mood they become. Their partner is determined to give them an orgasm, and they know just as surely that they are too conscious of his efforts and their own lack of arousal. They are ready for this to be over, which is not exactly the sentiment you want when you are making love!

The guy is aroused and attentive a lot longer

It's also true that a lot of men can't make love endlessly; they are going to get too aroused (or too tired) and they are going to have an orgasm. The thought going on in most of their heads is how am I going to get her to have an orgasm before I have mine? They are distracted or trying to distract themselves so they can please their partner, which means a real connection may not happen between the two of them. If they are taking turns giving each other sexual attention, each person can more easily concentrate on the other. Once they are both having intercourse, however, they get lost in their own agenda or arousal and they can't really do a great job for their partner.

The woman is likely to have a much bigger orgasm

Men, please just accept this. Most women will have their strongest, most amazing orgasms with a vibrator, dildo, oral sex, and/or by digital stimulation. Intercourse is wonderful and a powerful bond between partners, but for most women, intercourse simply doesn't touch the places that need to be stimulated. While some sex researchers believe there is a "G spot," an extra-sensitive part of the vaginal wall behind the pubic bone that is a key for some women's extreme arousal and orgasm, other sex researchers don't think it exists. If it is a reality, at least in some women, it is touched by experimenting with angles of the penis during intercourse or by some wonderfully designed dildos that seem to get at just the right place (personally, I think the dildo is the better bet). About a third of women never come during intercourse, and many of the women who do have orgasms this way have pale copies of the orgasm they get when a diligent lover directly stimulates their clitoris, and/or uses one of the sex toys I've just mentioned. It's not that women don't love intercourse; they may yearn to have their man inside of them. But as exciting as that is, usually the stimulation that builds to orgasm is caused by the penis pulling on the lips of the vagina and thereby arousing the clitoris, or by pressure on the clitoris when their partner's pubic bone presses against theirs. Why not just stroke the clitoris more directly when the woman is getting close to an orgasm—and save intercourse for foreplay?

Great oral sex, which everyone loves

There is simply not enough oral sex in the world. More is better. Done well is better than done ignorantly. This should be a feminist slogan. Done well, it is mind-bendingly erotic; done not at all, it's a real loss. Done ambivalently or without knowledge of a woman's physiology is almost as bad. If intercourse is not on the menu occasionally, this opens the way for oral sex to become more of a specialty and a more common act for men and women to provide for each other. More oral sex will endear partners to each other; it may not prevent divorces and breakups but, on the other hand, it is very hard to leave someone who really has talent in this particular arena.

Without intercourse you are more likely to play around with inventive alternatives, such as fantasy and sex toys

There is nothing about intercourse that means you can't use fantasy games and sex toys, but I bet if there were data on this (as far as I know, there is not), you would find a correlation: the more foreplay people use instead of intercourse, the more imaginative their sexual games. And I think this is important; in fact, I'd like to take a small moment of your time and write an ode to fantasy and how important it can be for making you feel intimate with your partner, for making you think your sex life with each other is unique. Almost anyone can have straight intercourse; it doesn't reveal much about your mind, your innermost fantasies. But when you share those fantasies, play-act them together, and experiment with edgy stuff like swapping genders for the evening or pretending you're strangers, you bond together because you have done something that you can only do with someone you love and trust. It extends the sexual relationship. You can have an affair, but just do it with each other. You can change sexes, but only for the moment. You can imagine submission or dominance. Try it on for size—and know that your partner will support you and not judge you. You can certainly include intercourse in these kinds of experiments—but intercourse can't be the whole point of being in bed together. The point of this is to have your minds penetrate each other's.

No need for faking—get your orgasm where you get it

A lot of women fake orgasm. Why? Because it's easier than giving the directions that would actually get them a real orgasm. Or because this particular act of lovemaking is just not going to lead to an orgasm, and they know their partner needs to hear them come before he can feel he has been a satisfactory lover. Women like to make their guys feel secure, proud of themselves, and studly, so they manufacture some convincing sounds and movements—and leave him happy.

But faking it often is not a good idea. The guy gets misled about what "works" and so does the same ineffective thing over and over again because it had been "proven" effective. She can't correct him because then she has to admit to feeding him all this inauthentic information. So she is really unsatisfied, he is misled—and neither is really meeting the other's true needs. The nice thing about forgoing intercourse some of the time is that almost every woman can really have an orgasm with foreplay. Then, if she has another orgasm during intercourse, fine; but having the orgasm first takes the edge and urgency and frustration out of the room, and everything from there on is just icing on the cake.

And not having intercourse all the time makes it a bigger deal when it does happen

Last but not least: If intercourse is rare, it's all the hotter. I know a woman who has a wonderful lover. When they shower, he soaps her up and massages her head, her shoulders, and every part of her body. Each time they make love he surprises her with a sex toy, an innovative position, or a new fantasy. Sometimes they go for a week without intercourse, but they have oral sex, use various toys, and plumb the depths of each other's psyche. She describes herself as "addicted to him." "If we ever broke up," she told me, "I think I would still have to go by his door and beg like a dog to still get petted." It is not a man's ability to last and last that makes a woman slavishly impressed with his sexual ability. It is not penis size and it is not number of acts. It is finesse: knowing his lover's body and how it works and playing it like a fine instrument. And it is having an erotic inner life together that is the couple's, and the couple's alone. Intercourse isn't the goal—it is just one of the tools.

15

MYTH:
If you desire someone else, something is wrong with your relationship

eese mate for life. If a goose dies, its partner will almost never mate again. But you are not a goose, and (we can agree on this, yes?) our species was made to be able to mate many times over the life cycle. It makes biological sense for us, given our long lives (and monthly female fertility) to be able to bond again if we lose (or lose interest in) our partner. This short, very abbreviated bit of sociobiology means that it is quite natural—probably biologically wired—for us to be able to look at and be attracted to someone else besides our beloved. Just because we are in love doesn't mean we are dead below or above the waist. However, it isn't mandatory to act on those impulses—that's another thing entirely. The ability to be attracted is one thing; following our eyes into bed with someone else is another (and another chapter).

Still, some people are so sure that if love were strong enough, attraction to others wouldn't happen, and they doubt the strength of their original love. They take this attraction—especially if it is a strong one—to be proof that their love is flawed. But that is stupid. A lot of good relationships have been ruined just because someone had a fleeting or even a real desire for someone else and thought that it meant they weren't deeply in love with their partner. They confess to their partner—who, upon hearing this awful confession, feels distraught, insecure, and may even withdraw from or break up the relationship. And some follow their emotions and have an affair, one that destroys the original relationship. Maybe the new attraction is real, but that doesn't mean that the existing relationship is flawed. We are hormonal creatures who need discipline and loyalty to remain in our relationships. We may love well, but we have to believe in that love and be practical about it—our body will always try to dissuade us from sticking with the one we are with! Let me tell you a story of someone who let her hormones, rather than her head, lead her away from a good relationship.

Rita had been engaged to Bob for two and a half years. He was attractive, finishing his medical residency, kind, and besotted with her. She loved him, and felt lucky to have him, but she was also aware of his flaws: his sense of humor was corny, and he had, as she described it, "no edge." "There was no doubt," she said, "that before Bob I had gone for 'bad boys.' Guys who are dashing and difficult. Guys who keep you off balance. Bob was there for me three hundred percent. And it made me take him for granted. Once we set the wedding date, I felt uneasy, worried."

About three months before the wedding, one of Bob's best friends, Mick, visited from Palau, a small island in the South Pacific where he had been running a medical mission for a charitable agency. Rita was thunderstruck when she saw him. "He was awesome. He strode over to my table. I couldn't help it. I was just awestruck. He was brown as a bean, tall, muscular, the most amazing smile. My heart was pounding. I think I was sweating."

She flirted with him. And he flirted back. Bob was oblivious. The trio spent the whole day together and then got together over the weekend as well. There was a palpable chemistry between Rita and Mick. When there was a moment when Bob wasn't there, Mick, a straightforward kind of guy, confronted Rita. "He said to me, 'What are you doing? Your heart isn't in this marriage. You are making a big mistake—for yourself and for Bob.' " Rita thought about it. And thought about it. Mick was calling her and telling her to come see him if she decided not to get married. Rita finally felt that if she was feeling this attracted to Mick, she couldn't really be in love with Bob. She told Bob the whole story, and they broke off the engagement. His parents and her parents were extremely upset; the couple had been together for six years, both families were friendly, and everyone had thought this was a terrific match.

To make things worse for everyone concerned, Rita did fly to Palau to investigate if what she and Mick had experienced was real. They were together for about five months, but Mick was better at courtship than commitment. He was totally taken with Rita for the first month or so and then he chafed at having her "invade his territory." He was a workaholic, and when he wasn't working he liked a lot of privacy. It became pretty obvious it wasn't going to work. Rita flew home, devastated at how wrong she had been, and tried to console herself. "I told myself that Bob had been wrong for me, otherwise the whole stupid debacle with Mick wouldn't have happened."

But today she doesn't really feel that way anymore. "Now I look back at the relationship that Bob and I had, and I know it was special. But I ruined it because I just couldn't accept being loved that much. And I was a fool for a stupid kind of passion." Rita is now dating another "very nice guy."

It's very easy to be vulnerable to someone else's attentions—or, for that matter, have your heart beat quickly if someone suddenly wakes up your hormones. That's particularly likely when you feel secure, when, unconsciously perhaps, you can afford to look elsewhere because you are not worried about maintaining what you have. But perhaps it would be better to recognize attraction to others for what it usually is: the effects of habituation—of being acclimated and unsurprised in a long-term relationship—rather than being mismated. Maybe someone else can stir your blood. So what? Don't take that as a sign of a lack of true love in yourself—or in your partner.

Allison and her partner, Danny, have got this one conquered. Danny is the kind of guy who notices beautiful women and likes to flirt with them. At first this drove Allison crazy, especially since she met Danny at a Club Med resort and saw him in action, leaning over every woman in the place who looked good in a thong bathing suit. She almost wrote him off as a trivial sort of person, but one night they talked way into the early morning hours and that was the beginning of their love affair and eventual engagement. Still, Allison was nervous that Danny was capable of going to bed with other women. And since he was often attracted to women, he seemed like a time bomb, destined to blow up their relationship sooner or later.

"But," said Danny, "I convinced her otherwise. I asked her, 'Did I go to bed with any of those women?' And she knows I didn't. I asked her, 'Have I ever been unfaithful to you?' And she knows I haven't been. I like women. I'm a social creature. And I like to feel attractive to them. But I'm not an idiot. I don't carry through with these little flirtations. I know that I feel an attraction to beautiful women, but I don't mistake it for love and I don't think it is any reflection of how strongly I feel about Allison. I am in love with Allison and I am committed to her, but that doesn't mean my hormones are dead or wrapped up in a box that can only be opened by Allison. You can notice other women and still be in love. I think Allison knows that my love for her is very deep and lasting."

And Allison does. She used to be tortured every time Danny was out of her sight. But now she believes in him. In fact, she admits, "there was a party last year, and I met this guy there who was absolutely fabulous: very smart, very accomplished, and very seductive. I dreamed about him that night and I felt so guilty! But you know, I understood it in the way I understood the way Danny could feel about women. Why shouldn't I be attracted to some swell guy? I'm a healthy twenty-nine year old; it's normal. It doesn't mean anything about how I feel about Danny. We're solid. In fact, we are getting married next year!"

♥

Attraction is just one of those constant possibilities between two human beings. The likelihood is that at some point in a long-term relationship one or both partners will fantasize or desire another person So, what should you do about it?

If it's your partner's wandering eye . . .

1. Note it and embrace it

Make it a "couple thing." A stunner walks by? Note the star quality and rate the person together. Use this person in joint fantasies. For example, Nadine and Richard, a high-concept couple—both in the design industry and both of whom are always dressed to kill—go to a lot of chic parties where everyone's apartment looks as though it's been published in *Metropolitan Home.* Nadine says, "We cruise the party picking out our favorite hot male and female of the evening. Then we go home and we pretend we are those two people and pick each other up." They admit their attractions—but use them with each other.

2. Give more freedom so that your partner doesn't have to choose between you and a romantic possibility

Allow flirting and don't jump all over each other. Allow some freedom with these emotions—in public spaces of course. Make a deal that flirting is all that will ever happen. That's usually the best part anyhow, and that freedom makes an understanding partner seem special—and secure.

3. Be playful—and don't be taken for granted

Let your partner know that you are not beyond finding other people attractive, too (and vice versa). You are both alive, healthy, physical animals who have given each other trust and commitment so that your relationship can deepen. But that doesn't mean you aren't attractive to others or capable of having a wicked glint in your eye. Let your partner know that your love is real—but it has to keep being treasured and won. Letting your significant other know that he or she isn't the only one who still has hormones isn't disloyal or fake. It's just a reminder that they've got something worth guarding at home too.

If it's your own sexual interest . . .

1. Don't give it more weight than it has to have

You can be attracted without making a big deal out of it. It's like dancing with a wonderful partner and not getting your head turned by the fact that you dance well together or by the excitement of body contact. Attractions are more often an artifact of the circumstances than of the person—and so many people can be fascinating for a short time. Enjoy the moment and understand it for what it is: a reflection of your ability to be interested and aroused—but only that.

2. Check out if it is a distress signal about your relationship

Are you feeling underappreciated? Nervous about an impending commitment? Your attraction may have less to do with Mr./Ms. Wonderful than it does with the fact that your primary relationship has some fences that need mending or has become vulnerable through inattention. If you are overromanticizing someone else, it may be because you are underromanticizing your primary relationship. Your attraction doesn't mean you have made the wrong choice, but it might mean you need to pay more attention to your relationship—or that you need to be paid more attention to. In either case, a little remedial action can go a long way.

3. Enjoy it

There are a lot of innocent ways to keep the juices going inside yourself and have that transfer to your main squeeze. You want to feel alive, attractive, and sexy. Sometimes there is nothing like the admiration of an outside person to stoke your internal fire; then you can bring home the sparks to the person you are committed to. The truth is that a lot of people use fantasies about others to enliven the day-to-day (or night-to-night) with their partner. This is a great use of a sexual energy—and there is nothing dishonorable about it. You don't have to mention these trivial attractions, but if you do occasionally and then initiate playful or passionate sex with your honey, your partner will start to think of your minor attractions to others as a boon to the relationship!

16

MYTH:
Never go to bed mad

This has been said so often to so many people that we have simply ceased to ask if it is true. The folk wisdom behind this supposedly indisputable piece of advice is that if you let things simmer, they will come to a boil. You will wake up in the morning, still in a snit, you will continue thus throughout the day, and you will find yourself even angrier when you get into bed the next night.

This myth is bolstered by a cultural shift that basically tells us to "let it all hang out." Don't button up those feelings. Suppressed feelings will fester and give you an ulcer and you will resent your partner if you don't get "everything off your chest." If you are angry, you will "let off steam," and the vision of that is like a kettle: if the steam doesn't escape through some channel, the whole damn thing will explode. So, of course, with this much scientific proof we believe that we have to work things out while we are still mad or our relationship will be hurt because issues won't get "handled properly." There is a rush to get whatever is broken fixed or, worse yet, to apologize and get it over with just so you can make nice that night. But of course, a quick fix is often, perhaps almost always, no fix at all. A Band-Aid is put on a pretty big wound and while it may look as though something is being done, nothing really heals. Psychologists say that one of the hallmarks of couples who are at risk and have a higher chance of divorce is that they have continuing issues—practically nothing of importance actually gets solved. Things just keep being put off until another time that never comes.

Trying to solve things at the height of anger is not going to do the trick. We have more to fear from expressing anger than controlling it. As Carol Travis has written in her book *Anger,* science shows that venting is a misnomer. The idea is that, like a vent, you can let hot air out and make the temperature cooler. But what scientists find is that anger builds up more anger. Instead of yelling and screaming and getting it all out of your system, what happens is that your adrenaline gets going, your heart gets racing, your judgment gets weaker, and your rage builds up. And for many people that rage does not dissipate once they walk away from it. Any small incitement brings it back to boiling in a second—a fact that is very dangerous when two people are arguing. This is the buildup that leads to physical abuse among some couples or, at the very least, the kind of adrenalized conversation that encourages couples to say things that they should never say and can never take back once the words are out of their mouths.

Of course, some people learned this style from their parents, and they don't know any better until it's too late. For example, Jill was raised in a very emotional family. Her father and mother loved each other but her father was an autocrat who, when crossed, and he thought he got crossed quite often, would say any demeaning or nasty thing that crossed his mind. If her mother kept quiet, the storm would pass, but if she stood up for herself the comments would get even more withering: "What do you know, Estelle?" or "You've got a grammar-school education, and a bad one at that. You're a moron," or "You should go back to the slums I found you in." Sometimes her mother would give as good as she got and call her husband an "ignorant, fat slob" and "someone people make fun of behind his back." But then the next day the couple seemed to do fine; so the model that Jill learned was that people could lose their tempers, say anything they liked, and then settle back into day-to-day existence. When she got married, she assumed that that was the way conflict would be handled.

And that is the way it was handled, but unlike Jill's parents, who lived during an era when no one got divorced, Jill's husband, Keenan, decided he had another option. He told her if she didn't treat him with more respect when they argued, he was out of there. And, true to his word, when she yelled and got nasty one too many times, he left. Jill was shaken and begged him to return. She promised she would go to individual and couple counseling. Keenan was dubious. He thought she was out of control, and he didn't want to experience her vitriolic tongue any longer. But he agreed to go to a couple of sessions, and slowly the couple came back together with some new understandings. The new rule was that when someone was mad, she just went to a private space until she got over it. If she didn't get over it for a couple of days, she wasn't allowed to speak until she could speak in a civilized manner. This was very hard for Jill to do, but if she was going to be married to Keenan, it was necessary. Over time it became easier and over time they worked out a way of waiting until she had thought about what was bothering her and why it was bothering her, and she could talk about it without raising her voice or calling him names.

♥

A huge number of people try to settle arguments in the wrong way and at the wrong time. They act as if there were some emergency pushing them to say what they want to say. But ninety-nine out of a hundred times the other partner is not going to disappear. There is time to settle these things and there are ways to do it that don't endanger the relationship but still allow for good communication. It is not cowardly or cold to wait. Sometimes people feel that there is something more real, more true, about letting their feelings out, unvarnished. But I say, don't mistake high-stakes shouting matches for a passionately honest relationship. And don't think the expression of anger helps you stay together: It is associated with higher likelihood of breakup or, if partners don't break up, with more depression. Here are things top psychologists such as John Gottman *(Seven Principles for Making Marriage Work; Meta-Emotion: How Families Communicate Emotionally)* and Andrew Christensen and Neil Jacobson *(Reconcilable Differences)* tell you to avoid—if you want to stay together.

Dumping or "sandbagging"

One thing that happens when people are furious is that they don't stick to the issue. An angry person is likely to try to hurt the other person rather than argue any specific point. If there is a lot of resistance, or they feel they are losing ground, they bring in every single thing that ever made them upset with the other person. When a person is angry enough, a conversation that started about sharing chores can end up with hissed comments about how lousy the person is in bed. Once a couple starts throwing everything at each other, the conversation is not really an argument about a specific topic anymore; it is an attack with the pretense of an issue. There is a surprise element here: one person entered the conversation on one topic, admitted to a problem, and then left him- or herself open to further allegations. This unhappy conversational ploy creates the distinct possibility that the attacked person will never want to open up and admit fault again.

Comparing

This is a tactic people will use when they have a weak case or when they think they do not have a shared vision of reality. They will compare their partner to someone else—with the partner, of course, show-ing up worse. In a calm environment people know that they are not going to win any long-term points by saying how much better a mother her sister is or that all the friends they have in common are a lot more sensitive about feelings than he is—but this is another crutch that people use when they are angry and they are looking around for any-thing that will nail the other person.

Contemptuous comments and contemptuous body language

One thing John Gottman found in research on how to predict di-vorce *(Why Marriages Succeed or Fail: And How You Can Make Yours Last)* was that, both early in a marriage and later, couples who were more likely to get divorced were also more likely to engage in contemptuous conversation with each other. Looking at videotapes of these couples, even the casual observer can see them roll their eyes when their partner is saying something they disagree with. They literally turn away from their partner, looking elsewhere when they are being spoken to—in other words, showing contempt for what is being said and who is say-ing it. When they do speak, the primary contribution they are likely to make is critical and contemptuous comments. Gottman says nothing is worse for communication, and I agree with him. It is this sort of thing when you are in an enraged conversation that leads to violence.

Not listening

This is an easy thing to happen in any conversation, but when you are angry it's almost impossible to listen to the other person. Each per-son is usually just pretending to listen; what they are really doing is marshaling their own arguments in their head so they can "win." The angrier a person is, the less likely it is that he or she is listening to "hear" rather than respond. And the more likely it is that both of you are just wasting your time.

Better ways to handle anger

The best way to deal with anger is to say, "I can't handle this now," and be honest about it: You are too angry to talk, reason, or think. That ought to cover it. But you have to promise you will deal with it in the next day or so. Don't be sucked back into the argument by arguing about when you are going to talk. Just promise you will and, if need be, turn out the light, go to the kitchen, do whatever it takes for this thing to die down.

Here are some other things that are better than getting trapped into dealing with an issue when you are white hot.

Specific appointments to talk (no drive-by snipes)

Make an exact appointment (tomorrow after dinner and after the kids have been tucked in, for example) and promise not to deal with the problem in bits and pieces. No cheap shots—and no responding to any, either.

Not doing it in bed

It's easy to ruin the bedroom as a safe place. Couples often store up everything and, acting on the "Don't go to bed mad" rule, unload when they are between the sheets. This is not what the term "between the sheets" ought to refer to. In fact, if you can manage it, your bed ought to be reserved for one thing and one thing only: intimacy. Communication, massage, sex—but not work, TV, or battling over anything. Keeping your bedroom as positive a place as possible will be worth a lot to your relationship.

Writing it out

Some people are more articulate than others, which can make the less articulate person anxious, angry, defensive, and, worst of all, reluctant to talk because it never goes their way. One way to help enforce the "Let's not discuss this now" rule is to start a ritual of having both write down what is on their minds, what their arguments are, what they want changed, and how they should go about changing it. Writing things down helps people express themselves—and it also makes it more likely that the argument will stay on track. Writing it down you look at your own feelings and arguments more closely and if one is weak, it is easier to recognize it and back down on that point. Writing also helps you see your part in the fight, rather than just focusing on blaming the other. After all, remember, the point is to get to a joint and satisfactory answer—not just have a complaint.

Watching your own body chemistry

The point of not talking when you are angry is to avoid acting under the influence of hormonalized aggressiveness. You want to stop talking whenever you find your temperature getting so hot that your fuse is short and your temper takes over. Most people are talented at knowing their own signs of getting out of control: shortness of breath, a quickly beating heart or pulse, general overall body heat—whatever it is. For some people, this can be an icy cool. Oh sure, you say you are not angry—but your eyes narrow, your pulse slows down . . . and you are ready to do damage. You may even be looking forward to it. In Neil Jacobson and John Gottman's research on battering husbands, the very worst of them, the ones who did the most physically dangerous things, had this cold remove take over their body during anger or hostility. If you are like that, or are with a partner who is, recognize it and get the hell out of there until you are in a different emotional space. Jacobson and Gottman found that the battering husbands whose pulse rates were calm and whose bodies showed contentment were dangerous because they *liked* the idea of the approaching battle. They were showing physiological signs of pleasure because beating someone up was pleasurable to them, not anxiety producing!

Taking turns

If you aren't angry, you might actually be ready to listen. Really. So give the other person all the time she or he needs and make sure you get it too. If you have your notes, you don't have to be anxious that you will forget something important. You can even take notes when your partner speaks if you want to make sure it's something you get back to. Taking turns, really giving someone the time to get his or her opinion out, goes a long way toward healing a rupture even if you start out quite far apart. If people interrupt each other, it can enrage the person who feels he or she is not getting a fair amount of airtime. Plus, the person whose sentences are being cut off cannot feel good about the exchange since obviously the person he is trying to talk to is acting as if she can anticipate everything and, therefore, knows everything that is going to be said before the complete thought is out in the open.

Making sure you were heard as you intended to be

We all think our communication is crystal clear—but it isn't. That is why Harville Henrix and some other famous marital therapists want the two partners to give each other some kind of feedback loop. I find the formal responses suggested kind of awkward and artificial ("Now what I hear you saying is . . ."), but I think some form of this exercise is really called for. Two people, if they don't check in with each other, can each think that a whole different conversation took place (that's why people write contracts in business). Assume that you are hearing everything in your own peculiar way, as is your partner, and restate what has been said and agreed to every so often. Otherwise, if there is a misunderstanding, someone is going to feel betrayed—maybe both of you.

Finding a way to say some positive things

John Gottman has videotaped and analyzed many sessions of couples interacting, and he finds that even one negative or cutting remark does a lot of damage. In fact, he says it takes five compliments or positive statements to undo the damaging (and anger-causing) impact of one negative one. However, now that you are talking without being angry, you can slip in a few compliments or positive and affirming statements. It will help get the conversation into pleasant tones and make it easier for each person to want to come to a good resolution.

A simple rule

The reframing of communication here is simple: What you say and how you say it has important long-term effects on the relationship. Conversations, even conflicts, have to be handled with care. The more hurt or angry you are, the less care, the less fairness you can bring to any discussion. Forget, then, the old advice about trying to solve every problem the same day it comes up. That is just plain bad advice. Wait until you have the presence of mind to use the skills that suit problem-solving best. When you wake up in the morning, and have had that cup of coffee and time for a little reflection, you will be much more able to deal with a problem maturely. And so, probably, will your partner.

17

MYTH:
You can never truly get over even one act of infidelity

I know that I am not the average person on this one: I just don't know why an act of infidelity is the deal breaker in an otherwise perfectly good relationship. If, as we shall see, the relationship is perfectly good, I can imagine all kinds of rather minimal reasons why someone would have an extramarital sexual experience that wouldn't mean a thing as far as the relationship or the person's commitment is concerned:

1. She never had had another lover and couldn't resist her one moment of freedom and experimentation.
2. He was totally drunk and gave in to a fleeting opportunity.
3. She was lonely and horny and her partner had been away at sea for six months.
4. They had had a big fight, were separated for a time, and he gave in to some vengeful indulgences—which he later regretted.

5. She ran into her old sweetheart from high school at the reunion, and well . . .

None of these is pretty, mind you (a partner would certainly be entitled to be angry and hurt), but they are hardly bell-ringers signaling
that the original relationship is dead or dying.

Still, while people will stay with someone during emotional or physical abuse, or when the fire has simply gone out of their connection,
they sometimes need infidelity to happen to make a decision to leave. I
am not sure why this is the bottom line. I know it doesn't need to be.
It is not, as the myth says, something that can't be dealt with. Let me
tell you about one case study and then go over the arguments that make
a sexual slip a bigger trespass than it needs to be.

Ned is a good-looking guy of forty-five. Tall, athletic, and high up
in the hierarchy of a national banking group, he always appears genial,
well put together, and in control of a successful life. He was married for
almost sixteen years to his college girlfriend who was a proper sort of
woman, a college beauty queen, and later a schoolteacher who took
time out to raise their three children. Over time, however, their relationship grew chillier and by mutual consent, once their youngest was
in high school, they separated. She asked him to leave their home and
he agreed. The decision, however, and separation from his daughter,
were very hard on Ned. He came from a religious family who were
very dismayed over his actions, and he felt a lot of guilt about it himself. He went to his priest many times asking forgiveness.

These visits stopped, however, when he met Loretta. Her children
went to his youngest daughter's school. He had noticed her many times
at parents' evenings. She was striking, tall, very dark, with masses of
long, black curly hair that cascaded down her back. He used to day-
dream sometimes of putting his hands in that hair: a guilty pleasure.
One night, after he was separated, he found himself talking to her and
learned that she was at the beginning of divorce proceedings. They

swapped stories about the atrocities of divorce proceedings and made a date for coffee. The relationship became intense right away, but not exactly mutual. Loretta was interested in a commitment early on; Ned felt unsure about marriage to anyone else, and Loretta was a real emotional challenge. They had hot sex but equally hot fights. There was a year that was full of breakups and teary reconciliations. Finally they married, but the pattern of intense disagreements and fights didn't diminish. There was always something. Still, Ned says, "I was totally, wholeheartedly in love with Loretta. I could be hating her and loving her at the same time."

About three years into the marriage, Loretta got pregnant. This was not completely good news for Ned. He had three children, she had two, and he didn't want any more children. But there was no choice since they were both morally opposed to abortion. So, they added a sixth child to their household. The relationship seemed to stabilize, but after a few years Loretta seemed distracted and restive. She started going away with girlfriends for weekends. Even more perplexing to Ned, she started going to dance clubs alone and music venues that were a day's drive away. They fought about it until one day she came home with much bigger news. She had met a musician attached to one of the bands, and she was leaving Ned for this guy.

Ned was totally unprepared for this. He couldn't believe it was happening to him. He was furious and drew an immovable line. He said if she was going to see this man, he wanted her out of the house immediately. He was staying with their child. Although Loretta had thought she knew what she wanted when she made her announcement, Ned's commitment to staying in the house made the consequences of her act all too real. She didn't want to give up her claim to the house, and she wasn't ready to enter into a protracted custody battle. So they both lived in the house; she stayed away from her lover during this time, and the best that can be said for the situation was that they didn't kill each other.

But their frosty cohabitation gave Loretta time to think, and she decided that she didn't really want to leave. On the other hand, she needed some changes or she couldn't stay. What followed were revelations about their sex life (it was terrible, and he hadn't known it), their everyday life (it was boring—he was treating her, in her opinion, like some dumb animal), and there were other things on her list of particulars. On his side of the ledger, he wanted an end to her mercurial outbursts and what he felt were infantile expectations of having everything her way, and he wanted assurances that if she stayed, there would be no other affairs. If she wanted to leave, she should just go.

All this frank communication worked. Loretta stopped acting like a spoiled child, and arguments became more civilized. They visited a sex therapist together and went to many couples' weekends for relationship enhancement and sexual growth. For a while, they tried experimental sexual encounters, even an experience with another woman because Loretta was curious about that. (They both decided that most of their experiments were better as fantasy than as reality.) They settled down to a more traditional sex life but their adventures, which might have been desperate and disruptive for most couples, brought them closer together. What it came down to is that, ultimately, they really loved and wanted to be with each other and they found a way to change their behavior enough to do that. It has been about five years since Loretta's affair, and both think their relationship is in much better shape than it ever was. This may seem like an incredible story to many of you, but I assure you it is not unique. It is one illustration among many possible ones to choose from.

If trust is broken, it can never be repaired

Like many things in life, what is possible depends on how much you want it. There are many helpful books (*After the Affair; Triangles; How to*

Affair Proof Your Marriage; and others) that can help you work through your shock, hurt, or anger. Whether or not you learn how to trust again depends, to a great extent, on the time you put into it and the willingness of your partner to give you the reassurance that you need. Others have done it. If you are dealing with a one-time event, it should be particularly amenable to being understood and the circumstances that made it happen more easily changed. The thing to remember is that trust can be repaired.

But there is no such thing as a one-time event

On the contrary. While everyone may think that most non-monogamy is part of a larger pattern, the data seem to show that the one-time event or, at any rate, the one-time affair, is more common than the person who has a string of names in his or her address book. It is the exceptional person who can keep creating parallel lives and supporting them. In most cases, the affair you discover is probably the only one there is. But even if that is not true, once you intervene, it is a whole new situation and past conduct may well be relegated to the past, never to reappear again. If there is commitment to the relationship, it is amazing what couples can do to turn their feelings around. If the bottom line is that they do not want to live apart, if each person focuses on how to stay together rather than how to get revenge, if the couple will take the time to find out what needs to be fixed between them, there is no question that the relationship can be saved.

I will never be able to control my jealousy

Of course you can. Jealousy is more about yourself than the relationship and is certainly no compliment to either one of you (see the relevant chapter, please). Anyhow, your partner didn't sleep with the whole world and if he is an adult, out in the workplace with plenty of privacy, he has had the ability, theoretically, to have sex with hundreds of people. But he hasn't, until now, acted on his opportunities. And to be more realistic, while your partner may be attractive, unless you are married to Tom Cruise or Julia Roberts, I wouldn't worry that it is only your presence by your partner's side that keeps away the hordes of admirers. It is flattering to be seen as desirable, but it is crazy to think that the emotion of jealousy is an immutable part of your personality. If you are a really jealous person, go to a therapist to get it fixed. It is not healthy and nurturing and it is not warranted, even if an act of infidelity has taken place. Real dripping, green, toxic jealousy is a mental problem—and you need to recognize it as such and deal with it. You *can* control it, because you can get to the place where you feel loved. Even more than that, you can get to a place where your self-worth is not dependent on somebody else's actions, even the actions of someone dear to you.

I will no longer be able to make love to my partner without thinking of the fact that he made love to someone else

I understand why this could happen for quite a while, but you can and must get over it. Your pain is totally understandable and yet it is not good for you, much less for the relationship, to let it deepen and expand into growing hostility and grief. You need to find a way past the pain, even though everything in your being balks at letting go of your feelings of betrayal. The imagery can even flood your consciousness, and yet is it really about the sex—or about the lies, the loss of intimacy, and the thought of the one you love acting tenderly and passionately with someone else? Wean yourself from the sexual imagery, spare your-self that torture. Besides, didn't your partner make love to other people before he met you? A previous wife? A first sexual experience? Something? Do you play that over and over in your head? That was then; this is now. You can get over this if you don't pretend your part-ner was totally pure until now and that your relationship is forever soiled. Just accept the fact that he used his body in a less than lofty way. The mind can still revert to his being yours and, if you have that, the intimacy of your relationship can be fully restored.

I am too humiliated to stay

And just who do you think is judging you? Your parents? Couples in all those other perfect marriages out there? If there is one continuous message of this book it is that no one should live your life for you. No one's opinion, or way of doing things, should overshadow what you think is best for you. Of course we all need to take advice, but some-times advice that's well intended is still not good—or even honest. How many people have said to someone, "Well, I would never take that! I would leave her in a split second"; and then, when the situation hap-pens to them, they stay! Would you like to be the person who listens to the advice of someone who doesn't even listen to him- or herself? Be real. Humiliation is a feeling of public embarrassment, but these days there is pretty little of that. People decide what is important and get over it, and so does the public. What about Hillary and Bill Clinton? If they can get over *that,* then any comeback is possible. The bottom line is that their case is not so far away from the rest of us: They figured out what was important to them, not to anyone else, and stayed on their own private course.

A few things to remember that might help you get over it:

Sometimes it has nothing to do with you

In fact, most times it has nothing to do with you. Maybe your partner needed to prove that she was still attractive, or there was someone so exotic she just couldn't resist the infatuation. There are a thousand different reasons. Even if, defensively, your partner tries to lay a guilt trip on you and say it's all your fault because you didn't lose weight or because you traveled too much, it's still rarely about you. She had other options, like talking about relationship problems with you and figuring out what needed to be faced and fixed at home, or saying she was going to leave if things didn't change—you get the drift. You are rarely the sole reason for the affair—but you might be part of the reason for problems in your marriage. The two are very separate.

There's no profit in staying angry

All you are doing is torturing yourself, and torture is never a constructive thing. Anger is almost always a toxic emotion—it is literally bad for your health. It is good to acknowledge your emotions: getting angry tells you something about how you are feeling, but it is bad to feed it, make it grow, let it become a part of your personality. If you do, it will make you unattractive to others and probably to yourself. It is altogether a big cost and its only benefit is as a diagnostic tool or perhaps an appropriate defense if someone is trying to lay a trip on you. But a continuing sense of outrage only adds a cost that you don't deserve. If you still can't seem to shake anger, go to a counselor who can help you work through your emotions and make your peace with the past. Try visualizing a new relationship of goodwill, trust, and renewed intimacy. Spend more time together and rebuild your pleasure in each other's company. Channel emotions into frank explorations of who you want to be with, and not into accusations and recrimination.

Sometimes the affair will get something fixed that needed fixing

Oddly enough, sometimes the recognition of an affair does more than tell you it's time to go; it tells you how much you want to stay and what has to be done to make that possible. Joint modification of a relationship after an affair makes the marriage stronger, more about what it should be about, and less about the things that have been bringing it down. No matter whether you are the offender or the offendee, once the relationship is faced with infidelity, you have to really decide if you want to stay. If you do stay, it is a powerful act. Sometimes nothing but infidelity gives the couple a drop-dead moment of truth about what their intentions are for each other and the future.

Sometimes nonmonogamy is what keeps your partner who he or she is

You married a wild thing, what did you expect? While the discovery of nonmonogamy is often devastating, it might not be such a big surprise to some partners. You may have known who your partner was all along, and it was that element of danger that kept you positioned on the edge of your seat: being your best self, having hot sex, keeping life interesting. If your partner is just the kind of person who loves ladies, or gents, but only wants to stay committed to you, if your security is not in question, is leaving the person you always knew he or she was really was what you want to do? Is it what you should do? If you bought a pit bull, should you be shocked if the dog actually bites?

I'm not saying that a person should put up with being treated badly, or made to feel secondary, or suffer any one of a number of unnecessary embarrassments, but nonmonogamy is not necessarily the worst thing in the world. And if you settled in with someone who had this written all over her, why are you suddenly going to punish her, and maybe yourself, for it?

What is it you are in this relationship for, anyway?

The bottom line is: What do you need most of all? If it is your partner, you can find a way to get over a breach in your sexual territory. If it is sexual loyalty, and that is more important to you than anything in your world, then so be it. But before you decide that something unfixable has happened, think really hard. There are hundreds of thousands of relationships out there in which one or both partners have been unfaithful, and they have healed because they wanted to heal. It may take awhile to accomplish that, but there is no doubt that Humpty-Dumpty can, at least in this case, be put back together again.

18

MYTH:
You should be prepared to do anything for the person you love

ost people think they have to compromise their future for love and marriage. People with common sense will tell you that marriage is a compromise (and then they will tell you that you have to "work on it"). What they mean by that is that sometimes marriage is so lousy you just have to put a pillow in your mouth to keep from screaming or throwing a chair. They also mean that in order to stay married long enough to keep getting around to the good parts, you can't be too obstinate about sticking to your original hopes and dreams. The message to women, in particular, is: "Love is everything. Give your soul for it. Go live in Sarajevo, if that's what it takes (even if it kills you . . .). Do *whatever* is necessary to make your relationship secure, even if it means giving up major plans, ambitions, or pleasures."

Is that the case? Is life and marriage just a series of settling for second best and planning for a future that never comes? Or do you think that even compromise is too selfish? That if you really love someone, you would want to do anything for him? That if he needed to move every year, you would willingly do that? If she hates animals and you love them, would you forgo pets? Or would you let your partner's crotchety old grandmother move in, the one who made his life miserable? Is this what love requires? The answer is no. Is that plain enough? I'm not saying there is never any compromise, never a noble act, but if that is the main theme of your relationship, get a plane ticket and it doesn't matter to where. Living life on someone else's terms for your whole life is a waste of your mind and spirit and body. The only relationship worth having is one in which you have the right to your dearest fantasies and at least a crack at making them come true. The only compromises that need to happen are the ones that come upon you by happenstance and health and tragedy, or are temporary coping mechanisms until you can get back on track. But if you don't believe this, if you think relationships are a series of getting only half of what you want and getting another half of things you can't stand, maybe you need to think again. If you are living more or less for someone else, and he or she may offer a great deal, you still may need to have your head examined. Let's break this myth down and see what we really have here.

Compromises that everyone thinks are necessary

Following only one career and giving up the other

It is almost axiomatic these days that one career has to suffer for the other, and in most cases it's the woman's. And why not? He usually makes more—and both members of the couple are relying on his money to build their lifestyle. But consider the lessons of chapter 21, about pooling your money. Dismantling your ability to make money early on in the game is just not a smart move. And second, remember the psychic rewards of a career versus the energy-sucking propensities of a job you don't like. When you are doing work you love, you feel alive and happier. When you are merely earning a living, you are look-ing for a way out. And the way out may end up on a dead-end street. It is *not* necessary that one career has to suffer for the other—or at least not for very long.

- You can commute between two close cities (and absence *can* keep the heart fonder as long as it isn't for too long or you're not too far apart).
- You can pick jobs only in cities that have opportunities for both of you (i.e., if you are into software, go live in Boston, Seattle, or San Jose; if both of you can't find a job in those areas, then at least one of you is in the wrong career).
- You can live in one place and then another—but there has to be a plan that guarantees that the person who lost on this move gets to win on the next, or the game plan has to take in both people.

Plenty of people can do this right. For example, Angela and Arnie, two peas in a pod in the fashion design industry, were happily making their way in the English design world when Arnie met someone who offered him a fabulous job in America. It was an offer that neither of them felt that Arnie could refuse—it was certain to lead to the financ-ing of his own label. But Angela was doing very well herself and had some leads about a joint venture for a shop on Sloan Street. They made a deal. Arnie would go ahead to New York and see if this thing was as good as it sounded. Angela would stay in London and follow her op-portunity. They would commute almost every weekend, he one week-end, she the next. Even though that would use up dearly needed cash, they felt it was important to be as much a part of each other's life as possible and then evaluate the situation every so often.

It started out great. Arnie's position as the right-hand person of a fa-mous designer was exciting, and it did look as if he would eventually be able to have his own label if he produced a few years of winning lines. Angela had found partners, and they had located a space that made sense. But they missed each other a lot—too much. After a year, they started to get really tired of flying back and forth. After a year and a half they were getting snippy with each other, and they decided that if they stayed away any longer it would be dangerous. But neither of them wanted to give up their dream. In fact, by this time Angela had invested in a store, her designs were getting some public attention, and she knew it was absolutely the wrong time for her to move anywhere.

Arnie felt he was on the cusp of something big, and he knew a move would be disastrous. They made another deal. They gave each other six months either to get the next phase in gear so that a move was possible or to chuck both enterprises and do something together. They reminded each other that they were talented, that if they weren't, none of these things would be happening. They realized they didn't have to be slaves at the whim of others. So Arnie told his boss that he wanted to know if he was going to be able to have his own label—and if he was, he had a plan whereby he could do it from London. Angela talked to her partners about how she could become less involved in the day-to-day running of the business and how she could contribute in other ways. Angela's partners agreed; Arnie's boss did not make a commitment. So Arnie, armed with the great work he had done in New York, went back to his adopted city in England and proposed a business plan to several people—and got a bite. Things were done on a smaller scale than they would have been done in New York, but they were done. And Angela and Arnie were together—and happy in their work and with each other.

Giving up dreams to have children

I don't know how many women have given up the idea of children, or another child, because the person they love didn't want them. I have known very few instances where this was a good idea. It doesn't sound important when you are twenty-five and the only thing that matters is getting the deal sealed with this person you are gaga about. In fact, often if the man is older, he may already have children and you imagine that being a stepparent or adoptive parent will substitute for having children of your own. That can happen. But more likely it will only seem that way because you don't realize how fierce love is between children and their biological or adoptive parents versus a stepparent who comes along later in life. I know, for example, a sad story of a woman who brought up her husband's children from eight years old on. She wanted children of her own, but her husband absolutely refused. He had three kids. He didn't want more. She made her peace with it for a while, and then a hysterectomy ended the possibility of a later choice. She consoled herself with her stepchildren—she loved them and they loved her. But when the marriage turned sour after a decade and she felt she had to leave the marriage, her stepchildren cut her dead. They would not talk to her or write to her, even though she had been a loving and involved stepmother. She was so totally shocked and heartbroken that she needed extensive psychotherapy to understand and accept what had happened. If she had been a lifetime biological or adoptive mother of those kids, the kids might still have been mad, furious even, but they probably would not have so cleanly chosen between mother and dad. In this case, Dad had the biological cards and Mom (as the leaving party) could be painted into a corner because of the protective feelings and reasonable anger that the children felt.

A child is an enormous loss if you want one and can't have one. And a child is an enormous burden if you do not want one but find yourself suddenly a parent. Childrearing has to be a joint desire; it doesn't work well to have to nag someone into guilty acquiescence or have an "accident." This is one area where compromise doesn't necessarily work (unless it's on how many children you will have). Men and women who have given up a deep need for kids usually harbor resentment, and that really reaches epic proportions if the marriage breaks up and then it's either biologically or logistically too late to start a family. Some women feel the loss so keenly that they have the sense that their whole life is ruined. How, then, can someone compromise on such a core element of personal happiness? No one should. This is one aspect of mating that should be agreed on early in the relationship, and both partners need to be dead honest about their feelings, priorities, and intentions. As one thirty-three-year-old woman told me, "When I met him I didn't want to scare him with an immediate declaration of imminent fertility plans, but I also knew that childbearing was on my agenda and that if it wasn't on his, I really didn't want to waste both our time. The really wonderful thing was that he was just as enthusiastic about living a family-centered life as I was . . . so as soon as we knew we were in love, we started making plans for a wedding and getting pregnant."

Compromising on lifestyle

I know of cases of people living where they don't want to, in houses they don't care for, and taking vacations they aren't excited about. Is there anything right with this picture? Where you live is not a small thing. It is the key to your mood, and your whole outlook could be changed. It's not a matter of money most of the time. I know people who are well housed for rather modest sums of money. People house-sit or they colonize a loft in a lower-priced part of a city, or they live farther out of the city and keep looking until they find their dreamscape.

But what if you have a different idea from your partner about what that dream house is, or what feels like a great vacation? Well, the vacation is the easy one—take separate ones, or alternate. But don't miss the places you've dreamed about or use your precious vacation time for something that is blah—or worse. Even if one partner has to live in certain climates for his or her health, couples can find ways of leavening that sentence. For example, Craig cannot be in very hot climates because he has muscular dystrophy and the heat is very dangerous for him. But his wife has always wanted to live in the desert. So, they have evolved a lifestyle of living in the desert during the winter and going to

Vancouver, British Columbia, in the summers. Easy to do? Maybe not. But it can be done, and both people get their needs and dreams fulfilled.

Sometimes you may not know how far you have strayed from the way you want to live, but you should keep asking yourself that question. Otherwise, one day you or your partner may look around at your chintz drapes and Duncan Phyfe bureau (and massive mortgage) and wonder how you got here instead of to the cabin in Montana that would have made you happiest of all. If you find yourself wondering why you aren't living the life you want, start figuring out how to do it. You don't have to live someone else's dream. There are almost always ways to do everything you both want even if it takes some ingenuity to put it together.

Personal privacy

Many people think this is the most luxurious and least likely hope of all. Time for yourself, unquestioned, private time. Women, busy with jobs, children, in-laws, parents, friends, and broken appliances can only imagine what a day alone, unbidden and quiet, must be like. Men, traveling too much already, blamed for not being with kids enough, dare not ask for private time for themselves. Too many people think that privacy is an extra they can't afford, and that their spouse doesn't have the right to any time that isn't spoken for. Well, you don't have to give away all your time. Just as the blood bank doesn't want your last pint of blood (that would kill the goose that lays the golden egg . . .) so you need reservoirs of privacy to stay the person you are and the person you need to be. Just because you live with someone or are married doesn't mean you, or he or she, can't reserve for time for yourself as part of the cycle that preserves your peace of mind and energy. It is not "extra" time. For some people, it is as necessary as getting sleep. And you need to decide that each claimant for your time will have to take that need into consideration. There is this old myth that the first time you will have time for yourself is when the children leave home. Well, if you don't take some for yourself now, you may leave home before they do! Ah, you sigh—but how? It's not so difficult. You could make your bedroom or another room off-limits (even for a question) for two hours a day. You could get permission to use a friend's home for a couple of hours a day while she's at work. You could take one night a week for several hours and go read at a café. There are a lot of options—you just have to decide you deserve them.

How to avoid the lost-life syndrome

So, we have decided that too much compromise is a bad thing and thinking that love requires handing over your life is definitely wrong, (and dangerous because you lose your self-confidence, self-esteem, and possibly your partner's respect; certainly a few years of this and you will, at the very least, be taken for granted—guaranteed). So how do we manage to keep the things that mean a lot to us? A few ideas:

Don't make a bad bargain to begin with

Well, I know that this rule comes too late for some of you reading this book, but not for all of you. Avoid saying things that you know you would not have agreed to if you were not drunk on love. (I remember once saying to a man I was infatuated with, who wanted to have a huge family, that I would love to have ten children with him! *Aieeee!* What love—or lust—can make us say! I meant it on the night I said it. But it makes me weak in the knees to think I would have ever considered it, no matter how terrific he was.) Well, perhaps you could never fool yourself that badly, but be careful of people who have large nonnegotiable visions—people whose idea of marriage is that they have everything all worked out and that all there is left for you to do is sign on the dotted line. This is not a union; you are just a beloved employee. Don't do it, no matter how good she or he looks. Pick someone with your priorities, basic goals, and lifestyle visions. Pick someone whose dreams match yours, or who believes in your dreams and wants to help make them come true.

Don't stay with a bad bargain just because you were infatuated enough to make one

Okay you agreed not to have kids, but now it's ten years later and you realize this is something you just can't afford to miss. Then insist on it. You cannot, and should not, be bound by a promise you made ten years ago. You are a different person and life is different. People have to grow and think and change, and sometimes a relationship just has to adjust to that. Call your partner's bluff, or test the depth of his or her love for you, and find out what you have.

For example, Cici was happily living with Greg, but she knew she wanted a child, badly. Greg was older and already had a child from a previous marriage; both the marriage and the child had not turned out well. The marriage had been an angry one, his wife was abusive, and the child had severe mental illness and had to be hospitalized regularly. Greg was still managing traumas caused by his ex-wife and family. Every day there was a possibility that someone would call and tell him his daughter was in trouble. She had been found naked in grocery stores or raving on street corners. He had good reasons not to want another child.

But Cici couldn't let it go. It was as important to her as anything in life. When Greg said absolutely no, she said she was going to adopt. When he said he would leave, she said she was very sorry, but if that was his decision, so be it. But when it came right down to it, Greg couldn't leave. He loved Cici too much. She had already started adoption proceedings, and when the adoption came through he agreed to marry and adopt the child with her. The child turned out to have various emotional and physical challenges that had to be conquered, but he took them on with her and the child flourished under their steadfast commitment. Neither of them has regretted making the decisions they did, even though it hasn't been easy. Cici did not give up her dream and Greg did make a compromise, but it was also an opportunity for him that he wanted: the chance to have a family that worked out.

Don't do anything for anyone if you wouldn't respect them for doing it for you

When you are about to do it all for love, take this pause: Would he move for you? Would she be willing to tolerate your friends from high school the way she asks you to for her? Is this relationship reciprocal? Is it fair? Are you asking something from your partner that is so much of a compromise that you would never agree to make an equivalent sacrifice yourself? Be careful that the compromises you ask of someone don't change your opinion of them. There are, for example, many homemakers out there who reluctantly gave up active, interesting outside careers because their husbands wanted them at home with the kids. But their husbands would never have done it, even if they hadn't had to make a living. And ultimately they don't respect their wives for it. In fact, fifteen years later this same kind of guy leaves his dutiful wife for a young go-getter in his office. Think that doesn't happen? A lot? Be careful what you do. Some compromises don't reap their just rewards.

Don't ever delay anything for more than two years

Some compromises and sacrifices are posed as just temporary detours. That's okay, but be careful that a compromise is just a detour and not a destination. There is rarely any reason for anything to be put off for more than a couple of years, and it is fair to pull the plug and demand your rights if you think you are being misled, either consciously or unconsciously. I have heard too many stories like Brandy's.

Brandy was a star from high school on. From a poor and dysfunctional family, she was determined to use her intelligence to avoid the ugly marriage and poverty that her mother and four sisters had endured. Her high school sweetheart was from a better social class and, recognizing Brandy's gifts, encouraged her to escape—with him. They both got into the University of Michigan and both excelled there as well. They applied to Yale Law School, but only Brandy got in. John did not. He got into his second choice, though, the University of Illinois law school, and so she stayed with him there.

That became their pattern. Brandy got great opportunities while John's, though excellent, were somewhat less stellar. Putting the relationship first, they followed John's lead, since Brandy was always acceptable to the places John got in to. Brandy usually didn't mind at all, though it was difficult when John got a job in D.C. and she had to forgo clerking for the Ninth Circuit Appeals Court—a dream job for her. Then when John got an offer back on the West Coast, he begged her to follow him one more time

Finally, Brandy asked when it was going to be her time. And John snapped back that she was selfish to even ask that question. He ranted and raved about what he saw as his great political opportunities where he was, and accused her of trying to thwart them. Only then did Brandy see that it was never going to be her time and if she wanted to take advantage of any of her professional opportunities she would have to separate from John, which she did. Looking back, what hurts most is not that she gave up some great jobs, but rather that John had never intended to be fair with her and was never as interested in her or as in love with her as she was with him. Take it as a rule: If you are asked to sacrifice for too long, your partner is not as much in love with you as you want her or him to be and you need to deal with that reality.

Keep asking yourself, "Is this the life I want to live?"

Remember, only you are keeping tabs on your life. Someone else may love you, but only you are the guardian of the terms of your existence. While compromises are necessary some of the time, the core of your hopes and dreams and talents needs to be preserved. It is a myth that love is best served by sacrifice. Love that lasts is best served by a fair and reciprocal partnership. And it is a myth that you can turn your life over to someone else and never regret what you have given up. Not only will you regret it if you give up your priorities; your resentment may also corrode the very thing you gave up everything to protect: your relationship.

19

MYTH:
Little annoying habits are unimportant in a long-term relationship

What does it matter if he chews his food with his mouth open? Isn't it sort of endearing that she clips her toenails in the sink? When you are in love, almost anything the object of your affections does is kind of cute. But when you are married, it doesn't stay cute . . . partly because you are no longer starry-eyed and partly because little habits, once indulged, often become big habits. But even if these behaviors stay just the same as they always have, you might find that they are a lot more important than you thought they were. In those tougher times, when the bloom is off the rose, small things can set your teeth on edge and accumulate into a drastically different feeling about your lover.

There was, for example, a revealing study done by Professor Diane Femly at the University of California, Davis, that bears on this question. The researcher asked people why they married and then why they divorced. It was fascinating—the reasons for divorce were quite similar to those given for getting married. The only difference was that something that had once seemed sweet had turned sour. For example, a person who said, "I married him for his incredible sense of humor" gave, as one of the reasons for the breakup, "He was always silly, he was a lightweight." Or another person, who cited her partner's creativity and spontaneity as part of the big attraction, later gave a vision of her spouse as "a dreamer, couldn't stick with any one thing, couldn't plan anything ahead of time." In other words, it wasn't that these people didn't know whom they had married, and it wasn't as if their spouse had changed—no, quite the contrary. The spouse was the same—but the charm was gone. Once things started to go wrong, all these strong characteristics became their mirror image—the dark side of the person rather than his or her strength.

I have an additional insight, too. I think that big tests of character happen a lot less often than small, annoying acts. How many times does your fiancé get to save your life—versus getting the chance to introduce you at parties? And let's say that every time he is called upon to introduce you, he flubs it, forgets your name, or forgets to introduce you at all, or says something inappropriate. Maybe if this kind of awkwardness only happened a few times in a lifetime it would be no big deal. But some habits are everyday issues, and even if they start out as odd but not yet irksome the repetition gets old once your hormones quiet down. Here's a list of behaviors or traits that most people tolerate in the beginning—things that would certainly not be thought of by most people as deal breakers—that I think might cause thoughts of homicide over the long run if the two people involved are mismatched when it comes to certain characteristics.

Personal cleanliness

What might at first seem like an admirable lack of vanity can be the forerunner of slovenliness. And things like weight gain, unkempt hair, dirty teeth, or strong body odors can kill the sex drive in a relatively short period of time. You don't have to guess that this happens—look at people's pictures when they are twenty-five and then look again at thirty-five; weight gain and reduced fitness are noticeable, even while people are relatively young. Of course we are supposed to love the inner person, and sometimes we do, and the outer shell really doesn't matter. I know a woman who desperately loves and desires her husband even though he is at least seventy-five pounds overweight. But don't count on this kind of devotion, and don't trust yourself to be capable of loving someone else "no matter what." I know so many women who, over time, just can't bear the idea that their husband has gross fingernails or copious nose hair. Usually the partner resists all suggestions to change—in fact gets snitty about any physical critique. If men and women don't have enough personal vanity to keep up appearances early on, their youth may still make them beautiful. But later on, every one needs to "watch it"—and if this isn't important to the person you love, be prepared to be disenchanted.

I have a male friend, for example, who over time stopped being able to make love to his wife because her personal habits turned him off so badly. They had met in the early seventies and were both hippies for a while, even living in an urban commune for about a year. But as time went by, and they married and had children, her disdain for ordinary cleanliness became more than annoying. Gerri refused to shave her legs and armpits, wash every day, or use deodorant. She felt that all these were cultural hypes because we weren't comfortable with our natural selves. Barry, her husband, had never been too comfortable with this philosophy, but when they were young, when he was mesmerized by her beauty, it all seemed to make sense and was bearable.

Then, over the years, his feelings changed. He wanted her to become more assimilated to a post-seventies culture. He offered to quit harping about the leg hair if she would shave her armpits. He even got her to agree to wash her armpits and her vaginal area before they made love, but she only complied with his requests irregularly. Barry became more and more put off. First he stopped having oral sex with her and, ultimately, intercourse became very infrequent. Finally, she very angrily caved in to some of his demands, but by that time he wasn't that interested anymore. They are still together, but both of them say their sex life is infrequent and they feel that each of them really has a "different sexual ideal."

Neatness and order

It seems like such a small thing—keeping things where they ought to be. But a difference in this regard is no laughing matter. Over time, a fastidious person finds piles of clothes all over the house unbearable. And a person who feels best surrounded by chaos can feel contempt for her or his more organized partner.

For example, Nina, a designer, married Fred, an accountant. She loved the way he took care of her. She was just starting a business, and he helped organize the business plan and keep things on track while she did the creative and personnel work. The business took off, and the marriage seemed like a complementary match. However, the same skills that made Fred good in business started to really upset Nina when they were applied to other details of everyday life. Fred wanted dinner at an exact time, he wanted the courses in a certain order, he wanted his daughter to do a certain amount of homework a day, no matter what, and he liked Nina to account for her monthly schedule months in advance. He posted her schedule and the kids' schedules on the refrigerator door so that everyone knew what everyone else was doing every day.

This was just too nailed down for Nina. She was Italian; she liked spontaneity. When she cooked dinner, the kitchen looked like a wreck, and she wasn't in the mood to clean it up until the next morning. She liked a bit of disorder. She was willing to be organized for business—but even then, she liked to have more creative chaos than Fred was comfortable with. Nina started to think of Fred as rigid and he began to think of her as flighty and irresponsible. This dissolved into name-calling, and ultimately they became convinced that they were two different kinds of people. This wasn't the only thing, of course, that led to their divorce. But both of them would cite this temperamental difference as a critical element in their ultimate decision that they were unsuitable for each other.

♥

It's hard to believe that these seemingly peripheral differences are really going to be consequential, but they are. For example, you may be like Sherri, who fell in love with Matt in college and rationalized all of his habits as simply those of a typical college guy who had never learned how to take care of himself. So she took him in hand. His apartment was a pigpen, and she cleaned it up. The refrigerator could have grown penicillin, and she would sterilize it. His clothes were in various piles around the room; she picked them up and pressed them. He ran out of soap and never noticed it. She bought it for him. In sum, she loved him and loved taking care of him. She never thought of his slovenliness as a big deal—until they moved in together.

Then, she started feeling trapped. She got tired of his mess. She got tired of doing everything, and she just couldn't live at the same level of disorganization and dirt that he was quite comfortable in. He was shocked that it bothered her as much as it did and thought it was a shallow preoccupation. They too, broke up. Moral: There is no right or wrong here—only the need for compatibility.

Too much or too little sociability

While most people know that they should be reasonably well matched in terms of liking the same people and having a social life that pleases both of them, they often don't factor in their partner's essential nature as carefully as they should. Many may know the Meyers-Briggs test, which is often used to create compatible work groups in business and help team building. One of the theories of Meyers-Briggs is that while differences in personality can cause conflict, they can also nurture creativity. Managers are encouraged to build teams of people with different strengths who, if educated to understand and respect one another's respective styles, will come up with better solutions than if they all had similar ways of working on a problem. How well this applies to love, however, is less clear. For example, the first item on the Meyers-Briggs test determines whether or not a person is an introvert or extrovert. This is used in a very specific way: Do you seek strength and wisdom from others when you are under pressure or do you move further into yourself until you feel better or know what to do? There is a scale of one to ten and, in general, you wouldn't want a ten and a one to try to put a social life together. Indeed, one of the big frustrations both men and women voice in an unsatisfying relationship is living with someone who, when troubled, can't share with her or his partner and needs to remain introspective. This is not a big deal to two introverts (although conversation might be sparse), but it is probably torture for a true extrovert. Or this same difference can be a problem in terms of how a heavy or modest social life feels to each member of the couple. One partner smooths life out with dinner parties, group trips, and family reunions while the other finds this all a waste of time—and deeply yearns for quiet weeks alone. The stage is set for recrimination. If partners can't find a way to have either the social life or solitude they need, they are going to be seriously unhappy. Ignore this difference at your peril.

Bragging and white lies

Confidence is great. And tooting your own horn is sometimes necessary. Part of becoming intimate is unveiling our past experiences and future dreams to each other. Lovers like hearing about each other's experiences. But over time, treasured stories get old. Worse than that, they get invented. Some people can't help gilding the truth a bit, and often no one is the wiser. But even though acquaintances and friends might not know where fact and fiction part company, partners do. And the greater the number of stories that get exaggerated and the more exaggerated they get, the more it rankles. In fact, when the bragging gets too out of line and the truth starts to get really mashed, it's not hard for respect to become damaged. This can easily turn into contempt. Eyes start to roll, grimaces are made—the exact signals that family therapy expert John Gottman says are harbingers of divorce. Respect is maybe the most key element of relationship stability, and small but unlovable behaviors can do it in.

To be fair, some of these behaviors are not small at all. Bragging and creating "facts" cause a loss of respect because they reveal a core insecurity that is not flattering or reassuring to see in a partner. These small moments are threatening because a partner's flank is unconsciously exposed; he is not aware that he is showing a weak spot in his character. And that is why these small acts are often so disturbing over time: They are too revealing. It is not just the behavior that is uncomfortable; it is having an insight about your partner that is unflattering—and the fact that she is unaware is so publicly exhibited.

Constantly being late and not calling or canceling

This habit gets old quickly, *even* when you are desperately infatuated with each other. Being in love, however, you excuse this bad behavior and accept it as just one of those imperfect parts of an otherwise perfect being. You get mad, you tell him to quit it, but he charmingly apologizes and gives you all kinds of good reasons about why it was impossible to call, why these meetings will be over with someday, and so on.

The problem is that people who are chronically late are being self-absorbed bullies, and they are being late with you because they can (after all, you have shown that you will accept it) and because they don't like quitting something meaningful for themselves even if it happens to be rude and dismissive of you. This isn't just a happenstance—it's a character trait. There is almost no meeting, or no day, hectic and even chaotic as some days can be, that doesn't allow for a one-minute phone call. And that was before cell phones!

Just imagine this trait over a lifetime. No matter how much in love you are, you will get the point: His time is important; yours isn't. And as that point sinks in, you will get increasingly cranky about the late arrivals and more than occasional no-shows. Sometimes this will be embarrassing, other times merely disappointing. But it will always create tension and often anger. I know one man who stopped going to dinner parties with his wife because she was consistently an hour and a half late. He was even more embarrassed when friends told him that they were actually glad he was coming alone because her late arrival had made it very hard to plan when to start cooking or serve. While this didn't end his marriage, it was the cause of more than a few really big fights.

Up too early or asleep too late

Sometimes people are simply on a different clock. One person is up before it is light out and has exercised for an hour and made coffee before her partner has opened even one eye. Or one partner starts to get tired at ten and has lights out at ten-thirty, while the other is watching the late late show at two a.m. Neither of these habits is wrong—but they are wrong for each other. The truth is that unless one partner can conform to the other person's schedule, the two people are never going to be awake at the same time. Or if they are, one will be disgruntled.

♥

Fiona, for example, is a morning person. She is up at five or five-thirty, and treasures that early time before her hour-and-a-half commute into New York City. She leaves her job at five-thirty p.m. and gets home for dinner about seven. When she arrives she makes dinner, sometimes with the help of her husband, Blake, and then does homework with her children and reads them to sleep. There is probably about an hour and a half that she has left after that before she is comatose.

Blake, on the other hand, needs his morning sleep and is never up at five-thirty with Fiona. He works about ten minutes away in Connecticut and doesn't get out of bed until seven, after Fiona has left the house. He has a much longer day in him, though, than she does. While she is thoroughly exhausted at night, he is full of energy and doesn't really want to go to bed until quite a bit later than she does. Sometimes he will join her in bed at ten so that they can make love before she goes to sleep, but then he gets up afterward and goes downstairs to work, read, or get on the Internet. In fact, he has become an Internet fanatic, belongs to several chat communities, and has ongoing relationships with two "pen pals." He said, "I am lonely, really. I am not so fond of being alone in the house in the morning and then, again, alone late at night. I am up almost always till about one a.m., which means I am usually up about three hours after Fiona is dead to the world. She is like this on weekends, too, by the way. I suppose I shouldn't really have all these Internet friends she doesn't know about, but I really don't like being alone so much and I find myself angry at her for not being able to be my companion in the evening."

Fiona and Blake have talked about this problem, but each feels that change would be impossible for him or her and would like the other person to change. Both of them knew this about each other before, by the way (they lived together for a short while before they got married), but they regarded it as a small annoyance and thought that each of them would like the time they had alone, that it would only add to their relationship. Actually Fiona isn't unhappy at all at the difference between them, but Blake really is. It's not such a small thing to him . . . and it's not a small thing to a lot of people.

♥

So what can you do? Well, obviously, the easiest thing to do is to take these things seriously from the beginning and see a difference in one of these traits as a big, flashing warning sign. But if it's too late for that, it helps to take them seriously now and do some repair work, or at least some compromising. Consider the following:

Create a short list of "must do" things regarding cleanliness habits

Even someone who doesn't care about personal hygiene can learn one or two new rules. Pick two that are really important to you and make a deal to change them. Most people are willing to do a couple of things to please their partners. For example, if it is body odor that really gets to you, tell your partner it is *really* important to you. Don't be politic—be serious. Get the products you want your loved one to use and put them in plain sight. Tell her or him what your libido needs in order to be able to function. Expect a defensive reaction but also expect some change. Unless other things are in trouble in the relationship, most partners respond to a serious request.

Make it easier for a sloppy person to be neat

If your beloved had good organizational habits, he or she would probably use them. If you haven't seen them, he or she doesn't. So instead of making yourself miserable every day, figure out a way to make it almost unavoidable to be neat. For example, keep dirty-clothes baskets *everywhere*—near the bed, in the bathroom, even near the front door—in other words, any place where clothes drop.

Hire someone to get the offending mess out of your sight, or at least make a deal about certain rooms being clean. Don't get mad and say your partner should be doing more. Of course he should. But he won't. Really sloppy people just can't understand what the fuss is about, and nothing short of a brain transplant is going to make the point. Look at chapter 25 as a possible answer: Maybe you would get along better if you lived in two separate places!

Create a model of a social life and live with it

If your partner is more social than you and you can't stand it, but he or she wants your presence, fix a calendar of availability. Figure out ahead of time just what you can bear and what she needs as a minimally satisfying plan. It won't make a social butterfly out of an ivory tower type, nor will it give a reserved person all the time he needs alone or with you, but you can negotiate a pattern that works. However, it takes planning. Looking at your calendar and actually counting how many outside engagements there are helps. Likewise, looking at what it is you actually do (how many social appearances versus getting together with close friends, for example) gives a better, more factual picture of your life to discuss than just this sort of general feeling that you never get any privacy or you don't get enough time with the people you care about. Come to a specific balance of alone versus friend versus "public" time. Documenting what you really do and giving each person at least the minimum of the kind of time he or she personally needs brings sanity and balance into the household. Otherwise, every week is a battle—and an accusation. No relationship can be stable if each individual feels as if he or she is sacrificing a large chunk of discretionary time.

Talk to your partner about her or his "exaggerations" and see if there are deeper insecurities that need to be dealt with. Until the underlying problem can be helped, use the time-honored "kick under the table" awareness model

Most men and women who have a partner who "exaggerates" try to overlook this problem, thinking that if they expose the situation they will have a fight on their hands that will undermine the relationship. But I'm here to tell you that if you *don't* expose it, your resentment will build, the behavior will just get worse, and you will lose respect for your partner. Take it on sooner rather than later (but take it on even if it's been going on for years) and tell your partner it does a disservice to him and to the relationship. Your partner might react angrily and deny exaggeration or invention, and it's okay for you to back down in the face of any specific confrontation. ("Well, last time you said you came in second in that race, not first, but okay, maybe I'm remembering it wrong.") But don't give up on the entire concept. Your partner probably knows she is playing with the truth and even if she doesn't want to back down on a specific item, she probably will concede that she has embroidered some stories. Be steadfast about it bothering you and work out a nonembarrassing system of curtailing this habit. A light, unobtrusive tap on the shin or an eye signal will alert your partner that you think the story has gone too far and needs some back-pedaling.

But this is a Band-Aid. If you think your partner's inventions are a deeper issue than the desire to make a good story better, then you need to deal with the substratum, the real reason stories get embellished. Is he feeling unliked? Unsuccessful? Judged? Uninteresting? If you can get to the bottom of this, you will be doing your partner and your relationship a real service. Like many of the other habits I have mentioned, a small offense may reveal a larger issue of personality or incompatibility. Leaving the problem alone may allow the annoyance to fester into something much more powerful and destructive.

Make it clear that habitual lateness is an insult and will not be tolerated

Do you notice that your partner is never late to an important business meeting or when she has to get to the airport, and that she manages to keep it together when something important is at stake? She isn't late when it will really hurt her—she is only late when it will hurt you, and you don't deserve this. By the way, if your partner *is* late for business or other kinds of meetings and is being professionally self-destructive, this lateness is part of a larger, more neurotic pattern and definitely means she needs some therapy. Otherwise she is well on her way to scuttling her job or career or advancement—something neither of you really wants to see happen.

If she is "just" abusing her relationship to you, and not in a total downward spiral, help your partner find some skills and some consciousness about being on time. Some things can be mechanical and utilitarian. For example, buy a watch that chimes at the time he has to leave in order to be on time. Make a rule about never starting a meeting after three p.m. so that she is given enough time to get home. Suggest developing skills about talking to the boss about a more humane schedule. Get a new set of promises about calling or canceling that have real penalties if not followed, such as doing all the housecleaning or taking care of the dog cleanup. If necessary, deal with the real issue below the surface—Is something wrong with your relationship? If there is a reason he is treating you with less respect than before or, if this is an old behavior, talk about your newfound need to be treated fairly and why you feel that way. This kind of behavior can be changed—and it's important that it does change.

Retrain your body

You know it can be done. Morning people can take a nap so that they can stay up later; night owls can get up earlier so that they are ready to go to sleep sooner. It's not easy—but it's not impossible, either. If people have radically different schedules and are starting to exist in parallel worlds . . . it's not a good thing. So start doing whatever it takes to be in your partner's world, at least part of the week. Synchronicity in this area is really important, not all the time, not every day, but at least for a preponderance of the week. Help each other. Wake him up with breakfast in bed or join an early morning workout together. Let her nap after dinner while you read to the children and then wake her up for a special dessert downstairs, or make sure she sleeps in on the weekends and arrange something really stimulating late at night. Partners may never be able to have exactly the same clock—but there should be at least a couple of times a week when two people can get in sync.

20

MYTH:
Everyone should cohabit before marriage; it can only help

I wish this were true. Intuitively it seems true and, quite honestly, it is hard for me to imagine advising you not to live with someone before you get married. I did it. My generation started the stampede, and now parents counsel their adult children: "Hey, don't rush into marriage. Live with him a little, see if it's right." Nobody, or almost nobody, is saying, "Don't live together. You'll be damaged goods." Or "Don't live with her, you'll dishonor her and you will be an immoral person." No, today cohabitation has become an extension of dating—a more demanding audition than just sleeping occasionally at each other's place and is sometimes seen as the last check for flaws before making a more serious commitment. The reasoning is impeccable: see how you work together on an everyday basis; see how you do "backstage." Put that way, it seems as though everyone should try living together (if only to check out their *own* mate-worthiness).

So, I hate to be the person to say maybe this isn't a good idea. But I have to. I've seen the research—in fact I've *done* the research, and so I've reluctantly come to this conclusion: Okay, live together if you want to. For some people it's the only way they'll feel secure about making a commitment. But if you do want an eventual commitment, don't live together *very long* because there is good evidence that cohabitation really does change the way couples learn to relate to each other, and a lot of those changes don't bode well for marriage. Cohabitation has many good points: You get a lot more time together, you can see if you are compatible when it comes to all those little things that make life pleasant or annoying (see chapter 19), and you get a much more realistic picture of your sexual life than you might otherwise. However, there are costs for these gains: You might develop a more cynical approach to the relationship—cohabitors are notably less generous with each other than engaged or married people. You also put yourself at risk for economic inequity—cohabitors tend to split things fifty/fifty even if one person makes a lot more money. And there's a strong possibility you'll spend a lot of time together and break up at just the wrong time—thereby sabotaging chances for parenthood or building a solid financial future. Read on for some sobering thoughts on prevalent misconceptions about what cohabitation will or won't do for you, or *to* you.

You can't really know someone if you don't live with her

Well, not to make too fine a point of it, but do you *ever* really know someone? I mean there are twenty-year-old marriages in which a spouse does something that totally surprises and shocks his partner. You get to know someone day by day, challenge by challenge, and there are issues that get uncovered in long-term relationships in due time, but you can't get them all settled in six months, or even six years. Living together will tell you some things about each other, but it can't tell you everything.

More insidiously, the person you are cohabiting with may be quite different from the person he or she becomes after marriage. Marriage and cohabitation really are different: Marriage is a commitment for life (whether it works out or not is a different issue), and cohabitation may be a commitment for a year. Think this doesn't make a difference? Of course it does. Partners are still auditioning, and that provides confusing information. Each person is unsure of the other, so there may be more positive and more negative exaggeration of personal qualities. For example, a person who isn't very jealous may be quite jealous when she is in a relationship that isn't secured by a commitment like marriage. The minute the marriage license is signed, she relaxes—and sees her partner as the most attentive of suitors.

A lot of what you can learn about personal habits can usually be found out on a few long vacations together—and a lot of time spent together. But time is the essential ingredient, not cohabitation. And time is a classic "double-edged sword." You need it to know enough—but you can have too much of a good thing. A lot of time together before making a decision is not necessarily your friend if you are definitely interested in getting married. Too little and there are not enough ties that bind, not enough veils lifted. Too much and, at least for many people, their data sensors are overloaded and can't function. The result is either a frozen relationship unable to go back or go forward—or terminal ambivalence. Read my next comment.

When you live together, you will get enough information about your lover's habits and personality, so that you can better your chances for relationship success

No, no, and no. Living in a cohabiting relationship seems to breed cynicism and ambivalence. To be fair, it may also be that certain kinds of people cohabit because they are less traditional about marriage and more likely to think of it as a flawed institution, and they might still be unsure of their emotions. But I do think there is something beyond that. I think there is something in the experience of cohabitation that makes it hard to know when is the time to make a choice, to change one way of living for another, and to say, yes, this person, with all the imperfections I have seen (not to mention the imperfections this person has discovered about me) is the one for me. In fact, quite a few research studies support my opinion. No more than half of all cohabitations go on to marriage—there are few lifetime cohabitations (few go on beyond ten years' duration), and in fact, partners are even likely to have a different opinion on what the purpose of the relationship is; that is, a lifetime commitment, a stage on the way to marriage, a convenience, or a great partnership but one that holds no promises about what the future will be. Unlike married couples, 99 percent of whom have the same idea about what they promised (even if they have different ideas on what they want to deliver), cohabiting partners are pretty likely to think they have the same understanding about what this relationship is supposed to be, but be dead wrong about the other person's assumptions.

Even more of an indictment: Data analyzed from the U.S. census shows that cohabitors who marry are no more likely to make a go of it than partners who did not live together before marriage. Sure, a lot of this may be due to cohabitors being less committed to the "till death do us part" vision of marriage. But if cohabitation is such a good sorting mechanism and living together is supposed to give you such good information about each other—why don't the eventual marriages of cohabitors just *shine*?

Cohabitation is good for couples because it avoids the old patriarchal rules of marriage. It is a much fairer, more egalitarian relationship

Would that it were so. But in fact, there is a lot of research to indicate that cohabitation is *less* equitable and egalitarian than marriage. For example, married men do more child care than cohabiting men! This doesn't mean there aren't advantages to cohabitation, however. Women feel more control over their lives and do have more real independence, and cohabiting men seem to do a little more housework than married men. But cohabitation is no panacea for gender justice. Most cohabiting men don't even pretend to share equally with their cohabiting "partner." There almost seems to be permission for a selfish, individualistic approach to life. And you can double those petty and unloving instincts when the issue in question is money. When it comes to money, male cohabitors, who generally earn more than female cohabitors, are not very generous with their partners unless they think they are building a joint marital estate with them in the future. Not that husbands are always princes about money with their wives—they generally use their greater income to have great power in that relationship, too. But compared to cohabitors, they positively throw money at their wives. Cohabitation is a pay-as-you-go system—everything has a label on it ("My kitty, your litter").

I have even interviewed couples in which the woman can only go on their joint vacation if she can pay her way! Isn't the point supposed to be spending time together no matter how it gets paid for? You'd think so, but people spend money differently depending on how iffy the "investment" is. So, unless she is earning a more-or-less equal income to his, the disparity in earning capacity is a constant irritant and detriment to the relationship. The relationship is rarely egalitarian even if she can afford to pitch in half of their expenses. In most cases, she has less money than he does, and so putting in half of their expenses takes a higher percentage of her total income. Couples tend to live at the level that their highest income can produce, and so she is often struggling to help support a lifestyle that is mandated by his income level rather than hers. True, cohabiting women often have more equality in decision making because they are paying their own way; but at the same time, they are losing economic ground in the long run. If and when the relationship breaks up, she is likely to be the poorer for it, especially because in most states she will have none of the economic rights wives have when a marriage is dissolved.

But cohabitation is sexier. Couples don't take each other for granted

There is some truth to this. Cohabiting couples do make love more often—they *have* to. Remember, they are still tap dancing, still trying out for the part. On the other hand, they don't make love that much more than married couples and, as is true of all couples, sexual frequency slowly diminishes over time. But let's say sex *is* more exciting. I believe that when relationships are tentative, the combined fear of loss, longing, and achievement motivation make fires burn brighter. So even if the motivations aren't enjoyable, the results are pretty awesome. Passion is kept alive.

We can agree that passion is a good thing. But what about this more solid fact that some randy cohabs aren't just randy for each other? The combined impact of lack of commitment, different definitions of whether or not this is temporary or a kind of engagement, and the fact that a lot of other men and women think of cohabitation as just another way of being single all combine to make nonmonogamy more likely—which certainly contributes to instability of the relationship. Unless you signed up for cohabitation because you wanted to keep your sexual freedom, the idea that your partner is more likely than a spouse to end up in someone else's bed is not a pleasant thought. But you *need* to think about it.

We can live together and then when we are ready for children, we can get married

But will that day ever come? Your partner may never be ready for children and by the time you find that out, you may be older than you wanted to be when your first child was born—or, in some really sad cases, women may have lost the ability to have kids. Women have to face the unsettling fact that quite a few fertility problems arise starting in the early to mid-thirties and the older a woman gets, the more likely endometriosis and other complications will occur that make childbearing less automatic. Most middle-class couples in America do not have children out of wedlock, and so cohabiting slows down the timing of when a couple starts planning a family. It is also true that having a child during cohabitation rather than marriage makes it less likely that that child will have a legal—and committed—father.

These are not small costs. Happily, they are not the necessary costs of short-term or intermittent cohabitation. But when a cohabitation goes on for a long time, and then breaks up, and a few years go by and then another long-term cohabitation is formed—again unsuccessfully—the timing of parenthood becomes problematic. If one or both partners wanted to be young parents, this may no longer be doable. For some people, any kind of parenthood becomes unlikely or impossible. For example, take the case of Marlene.

Marlene was always an ambitious and adventurous woman—but she never thought that experiencing a lot of life's opportunities would make having children unlikely someday. She had grown up in a wealthy southern family and while her own parents had such a dysfunctional marriage that she left home as soon as she could, she always thought that she would eventually marry and have a family. Still, at Louisiana State University in the early seventies, the world seemed like one big party. She had a lot of boyfriends and was high on "purple passion" punch at least once a week. She had a serious side, though: She loved politics. She ran for student office, became a campus activist, and, after taking some summer jobs helping out on political campaigns, decided to go to law school on the East Coast.

She became more intense about her studies—and she also stopped sleeping around and concentrated on the dashing student she had met the first day of class: Peter, an intense, narcissistic, and politically canny guy from Brooklyn. Peter was completely different from her: Jewish, from a lower-middle-class family, and not into any kind of frivolous entertainment. He was also extraordinarily handsome and was well known for his activism—he was part of a group at Harvard that was going to reform the law so that it would better protect the poor and powerless. Marlene was totally infatuated with Peter and, as had so many other women, sculpted her life so that it would fit with his. Marlene realized that this handsome, brilliant, and not surprisingly, conceited guy would be hard to corral—but she set herself to the task. She did extremely well. Marlene was also very charismatic. Very tall, slim, with angular features, a keen mind, and a soft southern accent, she too was the object of many of her classmates' fantasies. When she and Peter started getting serious about each other, everyone gossiped about the "power couple."

She moved in with Peter little by little, so that they were really living together before they had ever really discussed it. First it was just leaving a toothbrush, then a coat, then a change of clothes, finally several changes of clothes and her stereo. One night, laughingly, he said she might as well bring her cats and her books over too. They lived to-gether happily until graduation from law school.

At that point Marlene wanted some commitment from Peter, but he was making noises about not being ready to settle down. Still, he loved her—at least he told her he loved her and asked her that if she believed in his love, why did she need more of a commitment than that? Both of them adhered to the ideology of the time: that marriage was "a license to abuse" and that they "should be together for love, not for the state." Both of them really felt those feelings, although over time, Marlene began to feel a little insecure and decided that she wanted more of a "bourgeois" commitment. Still, she didn't push. Neither of them wanted children at that time, and he wanted to work on a Senate campaign on the West Coast. He asked Marlene to come with him, and although this completely mixed a job offer of her own, she went.

Marlene liked Los Angeles. She was resourceful and found a great job heading up an important referendum campaign, and they both were very happy in their new digs even though some of Peter's late nights and campaign trips made her lonely and anxious. He was often cold, vague, and defensive when she tried to tie him down about his whereabouts. When one of her friends finally told her that she thought Peter was having a fling with the candidate's wife, Marlene was hurt and furious, but not exactly shocked. There was a big fight, lots of tears, a separation—and ultimately a reconciliation. They were happy for another year until Peter got involved with a woman at the law firm he had just joined—and that affair ended their relationship. They had been together for almost six years.

Marlene was very upset about the breakup. She had loved Peter deeply, and he had set a romantic standard for her that she found hard to duplicate. She threw herself into her work and began to be recognized as an original, exceptional legal strategist. She took a top government job in Washington. She didn't date at all the first year—not that she wasn't asked. She was very attractive, and she came in contact with a lot of men. But it took her a long time to get over Peter.

When she was thirty-two she met Lionel, a tall middle-aged man just getting out of his first marriage. Lionel was still married when they met—he was a principal in a lobbying firm and had come over to the Hill and met her in her new job as administrative assistant for a congressman. They had several necessary meetings over the issues—and then they both began to invent reasons to see each other; finally, they just started dating.

It took Lionel a lot longer to get out of his marriage than he thought it would—eight months longer—and by that time Marlene was getting very upset. Even after he got out, it took even more time for him to feel comfortable introducing her to his children; almost two years went by, and she couldn't get him to take that final step. Finally, she issued an ultimatum: Either he integrate her into his whole life or she was leaving. He equivocated, they broke up, they made up, got back together, and they tried to have a relationship that included his children. However, the children were resentful, and Marlene continued to feel that his family, not her, came first. Finally, when she turned thirty-seven, they broke up over the issue of marriage and having a family of their own.

Marlene felt cheated. She was so angry and disillusioned that she thought she would never fall in love again. But a year later she did—this time with Andrew, a man she had known a little in college who had moved to D.C. to practice law. Andrew loved her totally, and they married within a year of their reunion. He wanted to make her dreams come true—and even though he wasn't that interested in having children, he was willing to have them if she wanted them. Unfortunately, her body didn't cooperate. During the last few years with Lionel, she had started to have uterine problems and was diagnosed with endometriosis. Shortly after she married Lionel, she had to have a hysterectomy.

I could tell you a dozen, maybe two dozen, stories somewhat like Marlene's. People cohabit, the cohabitations don't pan out—time passes and then something, often biology, gets in the way of ultimately having a family. Cohabitation just pushes the clock further and further ahead—and since so many of these living-together relationships don't result in a commitment, age starts to complicate childbearing.

Some tips about cohabitation

So, do I think people should never cohabit? No. I think it is irresistible for most people. If I were single, I don't think I could marry without something of a trial run. But here are some guidelines that I think can help modify the possible bad impact of cohabitation.

If you eventually hope for marriage, don't live together for over a year

Let's be real. You know everything you need to know by then and if you think you don't, you are kidding yourself. Bite the bullet; if you want to get married and your partner won't commit, get out. He will either miss you so much that he will come back on your terms, or he won't—in which case, you really didn't want this person anyhow.

When you cohabit, share and work as a team. Mirror marriage as much as possible

Don't create a model built on selfish individualism. You can have an egalitarian relationship with a lot of freedom, independence, and mutual respect without being chintzy or ungenerous with each other. Remember, you build up habits during cohabitation that don't necessarily go away when you marry. Act in a way that makes you proud of yourself.

Have a goal and make sure it is shared. Don't live on hopes, assumptions, or crumbs

Sometimes a partner is very clear about what she wants, and we just don't want to hear it. But listen closely and believe your partner. If she says she isn't ready for marriage—or never wants to marry—believe her. If you want someone who is faithful, watch what she does during cohabitation—and use that as a guide: People don't metamorphose just because there has been a wedding ceremony. If you are getting less than you need, don't settle for it for too long. Even if you do get married, you might end up with exactly the same crumbs. Believe what you see and feel and not what you hope for. Be clear about what it is you want. Just be sure you share your own goals, or lack of goals, with your partner as honestly as you would want to get feedback yourself. Remember that whatever your intentions, or your partner's, time will tell you what you need to know. Living together is just one way of giving each other the time to truly know each other. If cohabitation isn't for you, there are other ways of taking the time you need to know if this is love or lust, temporary or forever.

21

MYTH:
All committed couples (and especially spouses) should pool their money

W ant to save yourselves a lot of conflict and argument? Consider throwing this assumption *out*. I know there is a lot of precedent for this: More than 80 percent of all married couples pool their income. But remember: All traditions aren't necessarily worth keeping. This one comes from a time when a woman wasn't supposed to have her own money, so all her assets were dumped into the common pot—and out of her control, forever. Putting all your money together is really a terrible idea. It robs you of any privacy (even when it comes to hiding how much the gift you bought your spouse cost!), it makes every big purchase (and even a lot of small ones) a negotiation—even if you both have enough money to make that purchase without bankrupting the marriage—and it adds a lot of mutual interdependence in an arena where some independence of action would be both practical and, ultimately, more respectful. What is this big deal about having a shared checkbook? Why not just divide who pays for what and make sure it gets done? Wouldn't that imply more trust and be a more efficient division of labor? Of course it would. Fewer men would control the spending habits of their usually lower-earning wives and as long as bills were being paid and important decisions were being discussed, life would be a whole lot calmer.

Think it can't work? Of course it can! Gay, cohabiting, and egalitarian couples have been doing this for decades. Some cohabiting couples often choose not to pool funds because they are not committed, but some prefer to keep things separate because they crave independence, even in a lifelong relationship. Women whose husbands kept them on a short leash in a previous marriage aren't about to do that to themselves again, and men who had a financially dependent spouse want to make sure that in a new relationship, each person knows what things cost and how to do her or his part in it.

But it need not be just these kinds of couples who reevaluate what is a good way to blend love and money. This option should be open to everyone. Remember: Pooling is not considered a part of the marriage ceremony. You can arrange your money, spend or save any way you, as a couple, decide works best for you. Don't we customize other parts of our relationships as well?

There are a number of reasons why you might want to rethink this whole economic togetherness mantra. But before I list them, let me show you how some people have redesigned how money works in their relationship. Meet Sheri and Alex. They are both in their late twenties and each was briefly married before. Both of them had money problems in their first marriages. Sheri felt overcontrolled, mistrusted, and demeaned. "I was on this strict allowance. Since I made so much less than Kazuo [her first husband], he felt that it was appropriate that he make most of the economic decisions. It didn't matter to him that I brought in a salary, too. He felt he was the financial genius and he was going to do our budgets—what we saved, what we spent—and make sure we didn't screw up."

Kazuo may have had financial talent—but he was a bit short on interpersonal skills. Sheri chafed under his constant supervision. "He knew what I spent on dresses and told me when he thought it was too much. He decided if I had done well on making our budget that week. This wasn't the only area of control we fought over but this was the most constant, the most obvious."

Sheri finally had enough of Kazuo's dictatorial style. And even though both their parents were appalled at her rebelliousness, she became the first one in her family's history to get a divorce. More than that, she decided that the traditions of her family didn't suit her. Sheri decided that she would never pool all her money again. When she started to date again, she insisted on paying her own way. When she met Alex, she presented a very different self from the young Japanese woman who had married Kazuo. "When Alex and I became serious, I told him I wanted to control my own money. I wanted separate accounts. He laughed and said, 'No problem!' That was music to my ears."

It was music to his ears, too. Alex's wife had been a spendthrift, and he felt totally stripped by her impulse buying. They had countless arguments about purchases—from small things ("like S&W versus Safeway brands") to large things ("I couldn't get her to save a penny. She came from a wealthy home, and she was sure she would inherit our retirement money. I was sure her father was spending it just as fast as he could!"). Alex's ex-wife racked up a lot of debt that just about bankrupted him. He was thrilled to divide his new household's money.

"We each have a quota for spending money, and we aren't responsible to each other unless one of us wants more than the usual top amount. We also have a certain amount each month for savings and that goes into three accounts—her IRA, my IRA, and an account for big things that we are saving for. If there is anything left over after all that, it's no one's business. We've already made all the decisions that matter."

Maybe that's not the way you would do it, but the point is that there are a lot of ways to arrange money affairs—and marriage or commitment isn't necessarily linked with pooling money. In fact, research shows that conflict decreases when people keep their money separate.

There is less of a feeling of being controlled, so anger is less likely to arise

No one likes to feel that her partner is treating her as if she can't be trusted. No one likes to feel constantly watched and judged. Maybe it's traditional in some households for the wife, or the husband, to be put on an "allowance"—but the very word summons up images of teenage dependency. Most women I have interviewed who have money-controlling husbands echo a friend of mine, Lily, who is in this kind of marriage and has complained to me, "I hate the snide remarks he makes when I have to come back and ask for more money. It's always something like, 'Didn't I just give you three hundred dollars?' As if I were throwing it away somewhere! Then he doles out a few more hundred dollars, and I feel like he's watching each bill. I have a lot of resentment over this, and I don't think it does us any good. I know he doesn't mean to be insulting—but I take it that way."

There is more room for private economic decisions that are not being made "behind your partner's back," so that not everything has to require a huge discussion

Daily life is hard enough—and many couples are thrilled to stream-line anything they can. Barry and Patti are very pleased with keeping their money separate and assigning each other different areas of spending responsibility. As Patti puts it, "When I listen to how my girlfriends have to balance checkbooks all the time and have these in-depth discussions about a refrigerator or a load of topsoil, it makes me nuts. I am too busy to check in on everything, and I would hate to be that yoked together on everything. We trust each other to do a good job on whatever needs to be done, and we both roll our eyes at each other when we see all these nitpicky little conversations that other couples have. We want time together for the good stuff—not Home Economics 101!"

If you or your partner wants to splurge, there is private money and the budget isn't endangered. There is less fear of each other's spending decision as long as the joint fund is intact. If you splurge, your partner doesn't need to see the bill— and have a heart attack!

If couples have different spending habits (like "savers" versus "spenders"), having money held in common is like two horses hitched to the same cart pulling in opposite directions. Of course, if there is very little money, there has to be agreement about how to prioritize. But if there is enough for some discretionary spending, it's really best to keep the prices private so the other's spending doesn't drive each spouse nuts.

For example, Frances is a gallery owner who feels she really has to look chic and successful for her wealthy clients. She spends a small fortune on her clothes to make the right impression. Sam, her husband, couldn't care less about clothes and every time he heard what she had spent, he went sky-high with indignation—even though she could well afford to spend the money. They fought and fought over her inclination to wear expensive clothes and his desire to invest most of their available money in stocks. "Finally," Frances told me, "we just solved it by saying each of us could keep so much 'mad money' a month and it was nobody's business how it got used. Of course, he can see how I use it, but not seeing it deducted every month seems to make the difference. I think we bought peace pretty cheaply."

Money management is rarely an issue

You may have read lots of articles and polls that say money is the number-one thing that most couples argue about. But it really is different for couples who keep their finances separate. My research has shown that when you compare all kinds of couples who don't pool their money with ones who do, there is no comparison in terms of how they rank money as a relationship issue. As Rachel, an accountant, told me, "You know, there really is no reason for couples to be inside each other's checkbooks. I reconcile the accounts of many couples who keep separate books, and it works out just fine. They just need to communicate well and make sure they are not making redundant payments and that both of them are keeping debt and spending within their means. But I find that most couples negotiate this really easily—in fact a lot more easily than the other, more traditional couples that I work with."

So what are you afraid of? Below are the reasons people usually have for pooling their money. But are they really true for your relationship?

We aren't really committed if we don't share all our money

Most people think that the comingling of assets and commitment are the same thing. They are not. There are thousands of relationships that have antenuptials (agreements to keep property and money held separately before the marriage as separate property after the marriage or other stipulations that hold money or holdings outside joint ownership of assets). The majority of these relationships stay together. Increasingly, as people end up in second or third marriages, they come with some economic security (or debts) from a previous life that they want to keep as their own (or that their new partner does not want to be saddled with). Does this mean they are uncommitted or not truly married? No, of course not. Commitment is a state of mind, not a balance sheet.

Maybe not pooling would mean ambivalence for you—but it doesn't have to. If the relationship is about love, then it should be about love. That isn't the same as ignoring the financial realities of building a life together; you do want to be generous with each other, and you do want to be fair. But that's not the same as expressing how you feel about each other. You can love each other very much, plan a life together, and still keep money as a separately negotiated plan that you both feel comfortable about. (Just be sure the agreement is as fair to the lower-earning partner as it is to the higher-earning one. Ungenerous or inequitable agreements are not going to help any relationship fulfill its potential or lifetime goals.) Ask yourself: Do we love each other a lot? Do we trust each other? If the answer is always yes, why wouldn't you consider making pooling optional? Or creating your own unique plan?

Pooling will make it hard to break up. Making it costly to leave creates marriages that are more likely to stick it out through the hard times

There might be some truth to this. A lot of people stay together because they don't want to lose the financial equity they have built up together. Or they can't imagine facing day-to-day expenses alone. Each person has enjoyed the lifestyle of a two-paycheck family or had a day-to-day life built on the expectation of joint savings and investments. If the relationship breaks up, one or both people will suffer real economic losses; so they decide they prefer to endure the relationship rather than change the quality of life they have built up by owning their home or other major financial achievements.

But that is a double-edged sword if there ever was one. Money may keep you together, but wouldn't you rather have that choice based on love and respect? Wouldn't you rather have a choice about staying or going, or do you think that marriage is so important to preserve that you prefer to feel trapped—or hold someone against his or her real feelings?

Now, if you choose staying no matter what—then pool your money. It certainly will help you feel that you cannot leave. But if that doesn't seem like the right choice to you, remember: Keeping your money apart won't break up a relationship—it only facilitates leaving if leaving is what your heart wants to do.

We will not be as close

You can keep money apart *and* together. Just because every penny isn't observed, discussed, or held jointly, doesn't mean you are not planning your financial life together. Savings, investments, discussions of retirement—all the really important things—still need your joint attention. You will have plenty of money talk and collaboration. Unless the relationship is having other kinds of difficulties, keeping some money separate doesn't mean you have a totally separate financial life and it doesn't mean a lack of intimacy. Now that would be strange.

Actually, I think that keeping your money separate helps you to be closer, more involved with each other. As I've said earlier, you are keeping aggravation down by avoiding conflict about money. But you are also building trust, respect, and freedom because you have delegated to each other responsibilities that each person manages as his or her contribution to the family's economic solidity. I have followed this pattern in my own marriage, and I have to say that keeping things separate has made me feel more like a team than having to work things out on a daily or weekly basis. I am the kind of person who likes to streamline obligatory household details as much as possible and am impatient with accounting matters. Because my husband and I have done our assigned financial jobs separately, we have avoided a lot of boring tasks and kept our financial conversations on big-picture items that are more consequential or fun to talk about. We live a complex life (we run a horse business together, as well as a household), and it is comforting to me that I don't have to deal with some of the ranch books, and I know he is just as happy that I keep most of the house accounts. It's more separate—but we accomplish so much more this way. I feel closer knowing I'm trusted. Don't you think most of us want this trust and mutual reliance?

What will people say?

People are conventional. We all follow conventions because we think they offer safer guidelines. Whether those guidelines are good for us is another question; there are few rules that really fit everyone. Still, for some people, the tried and traditional is the best choice, and there is no reason not to pool money if that is what makes them secure and works best for them. Unfortunately, people don't pick only for themselves; many people feel that if they do something, *everyone else has to do it too!* It's an odd, but human, characteristic: Not only do we like to be in a herd, we also feel uncomfortable if anyone wants to be outside it.

So of course there is some criticism if you do something unconventional like not pooling your money. Parents in particular get worried that you are not really "doing marriage" or being "committed." They may worry about your spouse's intentions and whisper dark fears about the future. Few of us are brave enough or strong enough to shrug off these remarks entirely. We worry: What if they are right?

But we do have to be strong, because they may be wrong—and if we cave in, we try to live their lives, not our own.

♥

Niki and Richard are a couple I know who had a bad reaction from their respective families when they told them that they were going to keep their finances separate after they got married. Niki's mother thought that Niki was marrying a "cheapskate," and Richard's parents were worried that Niki wasn't really committed to their son. Niki and Richard felt that it wasn't worth alienating everyone, and backed away from their original plan. But, said Richard, "we really got in more trouble trying to do it their way. Niki felt that I was looking over her shoulder, she didn't like the way I kept our joint checkbook, and we got into arguments over spending that never happened when we were dating or engaged. Without broadcasting it to our families, we opened up additional accounts and redivided our money into household and personal accounts. We've been doing it that way ever since, and we are a lot happier. A couple of years ago, Niki told her mother about how we do it, and by that time her parents were less nervous about our relationship and didn't come down so hard on us."

Bottom line: Don't worry about what other people impute to you. Money can be managed in a number of ways. Pick out the one that causes the fewest problems and that best meets your emotional and practical needs.

22

MYTH:
You should always be one hundred percent honest with your partner

Every book on love—no, every book—tells you about the glories of being honest. Hundreds of movies will have as their theme, in some form or other, that honesty is the best policy; and if you don't believe it at the beginning of the movie, you do at the end when the boy loses the girl because he lied to her. It would be boring recounting plot after plot in which dishonesty ruined the relationship. It is taken as a modern mantra that a good relationship requires total honesty and that once honesty is broken, trust is gone and then, well, how can love survive? In case you haven't heard all the arguments for honesty, I will list some of the more common ones—and then I hope to rip them to shreds! Or at least make a few points about why you ought not to buy this morality myth as whole cloth. Here are how the myths go:

Honesty is important because it builds intimacy

That's true. It is wonderful to unburden yourself and let someone see the "real" you. If you can tell her everything and it doesn't harm the relationship, it probably will be a tighter partnership. On the other hand, rarely is everything shared without a price tag attached. When someone says she wants to know everything, she usually means everything she likes, everything she can handle. She doesn't, in her heart, want to find out that you used to be a bookie. Even if you think she can handle it, she probably can't.

For example, many years ago I was dating a guy. One night I realized something was strange; this guy shaved his legs! Because I had dated a competitive swimmer, it occurred to me that this could be the reason. Given his build, however, I didn't think so. So I asked. He looked almost relieved and told me he would tell me about it because being a sex expert, I would understand. I didn't like the sound of that and told him he really didn't have to tell me anything. No, he insisted, he wanted to be open and honest with me. So he told me that the reason he shaved his legs was that sometimes he liked to dress up like a woman and go to bars and pass as one. Uh-oh. Now, I could find that very interesting in an interview situation studying sexual identity and I could have a friend who dressed up and passed as a woman, no problem. But every little bit of sexual energy in my body went south when I heard that, and there was nothing I could do about it. End of relationship. Moral of story: I don't care how liberal someone appears to be. Unless you need to tell someone something because the relationship is going to a new stage and this is a key bit of information she must have, stifle yourself. (In this case, if this guy and I had been getting serious I would certainly have been grateful to get the truth—but I still would have been out of there pretty damn quickly.)

Honesty is important because it builds trust

Well, here is one place where the cost of intimacy often surfaces. You've told her about how, at the end of your marriage, when everything was going bad, you had an affair with someone at work. She was very sympathetic. But now she is your fiancée and she is worried every time you work late, or every time you introduce her to a good-looking female colleague. Or you told her about that youthful experimentation with homosexuality. Now you can't put an arm around a friend. Did honesty build trust? Nope. Honesty bred suspicion, and now you have to live with it as long as the relationship exists. Secrets, once spoken, can't be put back in the box. People just can't forget important information, and sometimes that information leads them to doubt you. Even though what you told them truly is in the past, there are a lot of partners who just won't be able believe that. Trust gets undermined, even though no one intends that to be the result.

Is telling the truth about every single thing the only way trust can be built? I don't think so. Trust is built on behaviors, and by making agreements on which you follow through. You can, for example, make it clear between you two that you reserve the right to keep some things private. You can omit rather than lie. You can negotiate a level of disclosure you both can live well with!

Honesty is important because dishonesty builds a lie that ultimately can't be sustained

I think you don't give yourself enough credit, or give enough credit to other people as well, for being a good liar! There have been lies that lived for generations. So what if they are discovered by a biographer two hundred years later—I call that a good run! Now granted, these days if you are famous or if you run for anything higher than postmaster, you are going to be investigated to within an inch of your shorts, but failing that, no matter how the myth goes, a lot of really big secrets get kept. That is, if people want them kept; usually the ones that get out do so because of guilt or subconscious guilt. Someone feels bad about lying and does something like leave a love note in a pocket or a message on an answering machine. Or she lies about something that is definitely going to be discovered, like an entry on a resumé that has her winning an award she didn't get or going to a school she didn't attend. Sooner or later a job search is going to blow those claims sky-high, and she knows it—unless she is so much of a sociopath that she no longer can tell reality from fantasy (there are those kind of liars, too, but we aren't talking about them; they are bad news).

I know of all kinds of important lies that were never discovered—and never should be. I know a woman whose child is not her husband's; he does not know, the child does not know, and no one is going to know. I do know of an exactly parallel circumstance in which the wife did tell her husband and, although they stayed together, there were years of turmoil, pain, and recriminations, with nothing positive coming out of it all except that the marriage survived. However, the boy was told who his real father was, which caused a lot of problems all around: The father felt free to meddle in the boy's life, and the boy was disappointed in who his biological dad turned out to be. Eventually, he rejected his biological dad altogether and only kept contact with the man who he had always thought was his father. So revelation brought a lot of heartache, and not much else.

Psychiatrists will tell you, however, that lies are corrosive; that they eat at a marriage and at the psyche and if they don't get spoken out loud they will cause damage. I'm not sure that's true, at least not in some of the situations that I am privy to. Furthermore, even if it is true for many people in America, I'm sure it would be less true if we gave ourselves permission, as a lot of other cultures (most cultures) do, to keep things to ourselves. The Catholic religion, demonstrating supreme wisdom in this case, has invented the confessional so that people can make a clean breast of their feelings, but to listeners they don't have to live with. This is the way to do it. Psychiatrists are the modern equivalent for people who don't have a religious institution to turn to, but unhappily the information, once flowing, doesn't stop there. Instead of taking responsibility for safeguarding a potentially painful secret, modern Americans think it is their duty to get everything off their chest—and onto someone else's. Many people who never signed up for pain (the man who thought the boy was his biological child was just a hapless victim in the ensuing saga) get a lot of pain anyhow. What would have been the kindest and most constructive act for the woman in this situation? Silently bearing the responsibility for her acts (and bearing the guilt as well) or scrambling family solidarity by letting everyone in this sordid circle know that they were wrong about one of the most elemental aspects of life: paternity. Failing some important reason, like a health crisis, keeping the family intact seems to me the higher goal. The woman's psychic discomfort seems a smaller price to pay.

Without honesty you have nothing— you're living a lie

If you are a drama queen, you adore saying this. But the rest of us think it rings a little hollow. What do you mean, *nothing*? Come on . . . you have what you have. And if you don't have some things on the table that you would like to have, it's the loss of some intimacy, but it's not the whole program. So your partner doesn't know about your hair implants. Does this really stand between you and true love? Does she need to know that those few, sparse, treasured hairs were dearly bought? Of course most people couldn't keep this burning secret to themselves; we have such a ridiculous desire to, as we say, "come clean." But it's not wrong to keep some personal information to yourself.

I know how strongly, though, some of you feel about this. I remember once asking my mother, who was married to my dad for fifty-five years, how she would feel if she found out that Dad had been unfaithful in, say, year eight. She looked at me with the intensity of all her seventy-five years and said, "Well, I would have to leave!" *That* rocked me! I said, "Mom, are you saying that the other forty-plus years after that wouldn't have meant anything?" "That is exactly what I'm saying," she replied. "I would have been living a lie." Egad! I am very glad that if my dad was ever unfaithful, none of us ever knew about it. Particularly Mom. Whatever they were living, it certainly wasn't some kind of charade. And if my dad had strayed, and been honest, I wouldn't have grown up with two parents in the household. I personally think that's worth a few falsehoods.

♥

Listen, honesty just isn't always the best policy. And in affairs of the heart, it may rarely be. Why? Here are my favorite reasons:

Honesty hurts—more than it needs to

Do you want to know that you partner lusts after your best friend? I don't think so (unless that would turn you on and your partner knows it). Do you even really need to know that they had a thing together before the two of you met? I know some masochist part of your personality would like to know, so you could watch the two of them like some neurotic hawk, but does this really accomplish anything positive?

I know one woman who grilled her partner for the details of his affair with another woman. She wanted every detail. He resisted, but she made it the price of staying together. So he told her everything, from the way they met in a bar to the conversation that set the evening up, to the details of what they did in bed. Every time he would stop, she would say, "No, you have to tell me everything." So he did. And she didn't punish him for it. Later, however, when they were making love, he would go to do something and she would say, "Is this how you did it to her?" He would get mad, she would cry—end of lovemaking. Finally she left, because, she said, "I couldn't make love to him without seeing myself as the other woman." Sick and senseless, if you ask me.

Everyone deserves some privacy, even if it isn't culturally allowable

You don't own anybody, and nobody should own you. Don't you have some part of your soul, some vestige of freedom, that you want kept to yourself, and don't you really want a person who has something left to himself that hasn't been thrown into the pot? Our society has gotten so weird about sharing everything that not only do we take away our mystery, a little of which is always good for the libido, but we also take away our personal integrity. Women feel the need to tell everything because they code that as intimacy, but sometimes men work better on the idea that there is something unreachable and unknowable that they can't touch. Granted, there are control freaks out there who can't live with that idea, but if someone wants to know what your thoughts are while you are in the bath, on the toilet, at your mother's—wouldn't that be a good cue to pack your bags? And women are the same way. We say we want a guy who is sensitive and tells us how he is feeling, but the Marlboro man still has sexual cachet. What we want is a sweet, sensitive guy who sometimes turns into the Marlboro man (except, of course, he doesn't smoke). This is possible—if you retain the right to hold things back.

You can build intimacy other ways—sometimes total honesty is an intimacy killer

As I hope I have made painfully clear, telling about past and present flaws is not always the key to intimacy. It may even block the kind of intimacy that you want, one that doesn't reflect on your weaknesses but instead builds on your strengths. If you have a partner who understands and is sympathetic, it is a natural inclination to tell her everything and sharing secrets is a bond. But remember: It is hard to know what the long-term effect of an admission will be. You put a lot on the line for an uncertain outcome. Pick a good friend for some of these truth-telling sessions—a very good friend, which of course also has its own risks.

All of this urge to create intimacy sometimes stops a relationship right in its infancy. Why people have the urge to be intimate on the first day, or night, I don't know. (Though I have done it. Personally I think it's all those hormones—they confuse you.) Anyhow, too much confessional largesse and your new admirer may have his ardor dimmed or, sometimes, shut out. Camila had had herpes fifteen years ago without having a flare-up since. Every time she told guys about this, even though she had been married for ten years in the interim and her husband had never caught it during those years of unprotected sex, her new beaus would disappear. "I finally figured out that I could be responsible and not tell people and just insist on condoms for sexual protection. I know they are not perfect but I was so tired of men saying good-bye. I met this one sweet, sweet guy and he seemed so understanding and I told him what I had been through and he didn't call again either. I had had it."

So much for honesty. In fact, just so you know, the data on sexually transmitted diseases says that this is one place where people *will* lie readily, probably because they had been through too many episodes like Camila experienced. Almost half will lie about diseases like herpes and a significant number will even lie about something as critical as HIV. Be aware that the honesty ethic is used when it's convenient. If you assume someone is telling you the whole truth about his or her history of sexually transmitted diseases, you may be in for an ugly surprise. Sexually transmitted diseases are one of those things to talk about on a need-to-know basis, but many people, pious about honesty in general, get self-ish and nervous and withhold information. Here's a topic where honesty should be required.

All this said, I do believe that there are times when honesty is required. Here is my short list:

Your partner's health is in jeopardy

You lost your mind at a party; you had unprotected sex with someone whose name you never quite learned. You are stupid and don't go to a doctor as soon as possible to make sure you are okay before you see your lover again. You are having some pain, some itching, one of those unpleasant signs that all is not right and you go to a doctor, finally. The doctor tells you that you have something lousy but not terminal, let's say genital warts, a type of human papilloma virus. (Maybe there *is* a deity that really wants to punish us for recreational sex . . .) You now have something serious that is potentially communicable, and you have to face the music—whatever the cost. Honesty is not going to be fun, and may even cost you your relationship, but your partner's lifetime health is at stake. You have to tell.

Your partner needs real feedback, and only you can give it

You can't take it anymore. You have faked your last orgasm or just don't want to be bored again during oral sex. You have to tell your partner what is really going on, or sex is just going to get more and more annoying. This is hard, especially if you have been faking enjoyment for more than a few months. But you can tell that you are really getting disappointed and that it is affecting how you feel about the relationship. Your partner deserves to know what is really going on so that the two of you can change it. (Yes, I know I said you can't perfect sex with an untalented lover, but if you work on it you could make it a lot better and probably at least adequate.) Or your partner's personal hygiene has been deteriorating. Or you don't want to hear your partner bragging anymore about the famous people she knows. Whatever it is, if it is becoming a burr under your saddle, recognize that you'd better get it out of there before you aren't rideable.

You have been a saint up to now, but your partner has been a sinner. You are way ahead, with plenty of credits in the relationship bank to balance a few deficits, so you can unburden yourself without much fear

You have spent much more money than you could afford. You know you shouldn't have, and you know that your partner is going to go ballistic. But you also know that she did worse last year and you were a saint. You have credits in the relationship bank here, and it's time to draw on them. (Most partners know when they owe their other half a bit of leeway; and if your partner doesn't see that—reevaluate this relationship.) On the other hand, demanding fairness doesn't work in some arenas of human connection: Just because your partner had an affair, told you, and was forgiven doesn't mean he will extend you the same privilege. Still, it makes it more difficult for the other person to give in to his full performance of righteous rage. The key here is that if you develop a reciprocal pattern of coming clean with each other and know that there will be an acceptable and a fair discussion, you can unburden yourself in a safe manner—and increase intimacy.

You don't care what happens

Sometimes you get to a point in the relationship where things are so bad that you are on your way out and the only thing that might save the whole thing is a slash-and-burn return to basics. You are tired of an entire alphabet of misdemeanors or maybe even felonies. You have your emotional bags packed, and the real ones aren't far behind. What have you got to lose? Even if it's painful, you feel the need to unburden yourself. Strangely, sometimes this does change things. Some people will only listen and understand at the twelfth hour, an unfortunate but real fact. But this puts everything on the line, so you don't want to practice this kind of brinkmanship unless you are prepared for this to be the end of the relationship. Unhappily, the kinds of crisis situations that invite large secrets to spill out often have people at their wit's end and the truth-telling may happen in traumatic circumstances when people are trying to be cruel rather than constructive. If you are telling the truth in hopes of reestablishing the relationship on better ground, you will need to use some restraint so there is room for someone to feel hope or retain dignity. If you can't unburden yourself with constructive information, if you just want to get back at someone and there is not even a small chance of fixing anything—why not just leave before taking your pound of flesh?

There is actually some good that can come of being honest

That is a pretty good rule for all revelations: What am I trying to accomplish here? What can I accomplish? Will telling her about what a rat you were with the five women before her really do anything for the relationship? On the other hand, if you know exactly what she shouldn't do in a relationship with you, or there are serious things about you that need to be accepted or understood or the relationship will fail, then those kinds of truth-telling sessions are very much in order. Marie said, "Gil gave me many long, painful stories of what had gone wrong in his marriage and parts of it were painful to hear. He had had a breakdown after his marriage broke up and had to go to a hospital for depression and alcoholism. He told me everything about that, too. I understood a lot more about what drinking could and would do to his life if he ever had even one drink again. He felt I needed to be fully informed about what he had been though and why he never wanted to be anywhere where there was even social drinking going on. We made a pact about that, and he has been as good as his word. He didn't feel we could have a real relationship without my knowing what he had been through and what he needed support with. I agree. I signed up with full knowledge. If I hadn't known everything, this never would have worked."

You cannot function any other way

There are some people for whom honesty isn't an important thing in the relationship; it is the *only* thing. A former assistant of mine, and still a friend, is an attractive, vibrant young woman, for whom honesty, total honesty, is nonnegotiable. When the man she was seeing lied about whom he was talking to because he didn't want to admit it was his old girlfriend, it threw the relationship into a full-blown crisis. Karla could not accept his apology for a long time because, to her, any deviation from the truth is cause for an absolute loss of trust—even if the issue itself is not grave. Karla needs someone who is one hundred percent honest, who can accept her as she is and acts in a way that never needs to be cloaked, evaded, or distorted. This has turned out to be a tall order, and there have been many promising relationships that abruptly ended or began to unravel when she found out the truth was shaded. She is incapable of acting or feeling any other way. So she needs to specify this need right up-front and find someone who lives and thinks as she does.

Pick your confessions carefully

Yes, there are reasons for telling the deepest and most painful things. But don't think this is an all-or-nothing requirement of intimacy. Almost everyone needs to leave some things unsaid. Make that everyone. But when you do need to tell, how do you know what your partner can handle? What cues can you use to decide when to speak and when to be quiet?

1. Listen to your partner
Most people will tell you what they can or cannot handle: maybe not directly, but you'll get the message if you're observant. If you tell him that a shirt doesn't suit him, do you get a huffy response or does he happily change it? If you comment on his mother's abrupt manner with service people, does he get thoughtful or defensive? How does your partner talk about other people? How judgmental is he? How forgiving? If you listen, you will begin to know tolerance levels and reactions.

2. Give a small amount of information and see what happens
Before you tell him about fantasizing occasionally about other men while you are making love, talk about fantasy in general and see what his opinions are. Does he think wild fantasies are harmless fun or does he think they are rehearsals, harbingers of things to come? If you tell him an unlikely person popped up in a dream, does he fixate on it—or laugh about it and forget it? Start slowly and see if you should stop entirely or share more.

3. Think about how your partner wants and needs to see you
Will you be shattering everything he needs you to be? What will be

left? If you feel you are living a lie and need to change, so be it. But if you *want* to be seen the way your partner currently sees you, think many times before you shatter his beliefs and perceptions.

4. Think a long time about dropping a bombshell, and don't do it impulsively

It is so tempting to disclose important things in quiet, sharing moments, or when the relationship is in turmoil and you feel like putting everything into play. But resist the impulse. Wait for a less emotional moment and see if the need to make the disclosure is still there. Don't make a sudden decision in a long-term relationship.

5. Know your partner and act in accordance with that knowledge rather than what your partner says

If your partner is haunted by any unflattering information of breeches of fidelity, her desire to know will cost her, and you, highly—no matter what is said to the contrary. Unless the need to know is undeniable, lean on the side of caution. If you love your partner and your partnership, discretion should be the usual, not the exceptional, approach.

23

MYTH:
Divorce means failure; marriage should last a lifetime

People give a lot of points to anything that takes a lot of time. How long did it take you to whittle that wood? Forty years? Wow. And just about everyone clucks appreciatively and smiles when couples say they have been together for five decades. Of course, all of them may have been miserable—but even if people know that they were awful to each other, they give them credit for sticking it out all the same. Everyone in our family knew that my paternal grandparents, who had been married for sixty years, disliked each other for about fifty-nine of them. But that didn't stop us from giving them a big, joyous silver anniversary party. Of course by that time they were so frail and dependent on each other that they probably forgot they didn't like each other. But it took them too many painful years to get to a pleasant truce. Which years were we celebrating ? The last two? Or all the really nasty ones?

The truth is that longevity in a troubled marriage is sadder than if the relationship had lasted for a much shorter time. Conversely, some relationships that last a short time and end should be celebrated because they were good for the people while they lasted and should be considered a success. They accomplished exactly what they could accomplish. Bigger is not always better, and shorter is not necessarily more worthy than longer. Sometimes one or both partners are holding each other back; they are stuck, destructive, and bringing out the worst in each other. Stagnation may not be dramatic, but it is a devastation of the spirit, nonetheless. When a long-term relationship is devitalizing or destructive, it is better to leave than to preserve an idea (marriage/family) over a reality (unhappiness/incompatibility). Let me give you some examples in which the end of the marriage should be considered an achievement rather than a failure.

The classic first love

Tim and Nancy fell in love their freshman year of college. Nancy was backstage helping with the makeup for the big year-end school musical. Tim was one of the actors, and she was assigned to put on his makeup. He was so handsome, she was smitten just about as soon as she saw him. He exemplified her ideal man: blond hair, blue eyes, and a chiseled, angular face. She was really surprised that he found her attractive, too. She was nice-looking but somewhat overweight and not usually sought by the "pretty boys" that she so coveted. But he not only asked her out; he was almost as immediately taken with her as she was with him. They got serious right away and had a public "pinning" ceremony in front of her sorority and his fraternity. When she became president of her sorority and he president of his fraternity, they were considered a "star couple" and everyone complimented her on how lucky they were to have found each other.

But as the years wore on, Nancy felt luckier in public than in private. Tim was from a working-class background, and he was happy to have made it to college and to law school. He wanted to open up a one-man office and have a small, low-key practice. Nancy was already igniting sparks as a journalist on the school paper. She wanted to go to Columbia School of Journalism, live in New York, and ultimately get a job at *The New York Times.*

Neither one really liked the other's dream. Yet they stayed together. Finally, at the senior-year mark, it was clear that some decisions had to be made. They had been together almost four years, people they knew were getting engaged; it was obvious what the next step was supposed to be. Nancy couldn't face the relationship being over, but she knew it was not strong enough to continue. "I loved Tim, but I wasn't 'in love' with him anymore. When I was younger, I desperately needed someone to tell me I was attractive. I needed someone good-looking to do that. As I grew stronger, inside, Tim's sweetness and love were still wonderful, but I needed more. I needed someone who was my intellectual match, someone who was trying to go where I wanted to go. Professionally, that is. Tim wasn't it, but I couldn't face that so I'll always be sorry that I backed out of the relationship dishonorably instead of just recognizing it was over."

Nancy had an affair. Tim found out. And they broke up, with Tim hurt and so angry that he wouldn't talk to Nancy until many years later. Only then, both living different lifestyles, could they celebrate what had been a very good relationship, the right relationship for both of them at the time, and not fixate on its unhappy ending.

The classic first marriage

Jack and Daisy were married in the most beautiful ceremony their parents could afford. Or almost afford. It was everything Daisy had ever dreamed about and even though she felt guilty that her parents had gone out on such an economic limb, she knew it was a day she would treasure all of her life. Jack looked so handsome and, true to his nature, he had made sure all the details were to his liking. She was in awe of him. He was so powerful, smart, and he loved her! She doted on him.

The marriage seemed perfect. Jack wanted to take on the world. Daisy wanted to take over the home and support Jack in his work. Their early years were great. Jack worked hard at carving out a piece of his family business, and Daisy made their home a lovely haven for him. They intended to have children, but Daisy had difficulty getting pregnant; after a complete workup they discovered that pregnancy wasn't impossible, but it would be difficult. Finally, when she did get pregnant, they were both joyous. But Daisy was so nervous during the pregnancy and then so dedicated to their new baby when he arrived, that it started to affect their marriage. Jack had wanted a woman to take care of him and be a mother to his children, but he hadn't really thought about how someone that dedicated to home and family would be as a lifetime partner. As time went on, Daisy seemed to be much more engaged with little Jack Jr. than just about anything else. She had never been too interested in Jack's business struggles, and she became even less so. Their talk became superficial. They interacted best at family gatherings, but time at home alone was mostly spent discussing practical matters or Jack Jr. Their sex life, always nice but not especially passionate, became less active and less satisfying to both of them. Jack started to think that classic question of failing marriages: "Is this all there is?"

"Daisy is a great woman," says Jack, now in the middle of divorce proceedings. "And I think when we got married we were exactly what we both needed. But we really weren't matched well in terms of intimacy. I felt so alone almost all the time. Daisy got what she needed from Jack Jr. I don't think she ever really needed to be close to me. I began to long for someone who was more of an equal, someone to think with, plan with, and someone with a sexual appetite like my own. I think Daisy and I were good parents and we fitted well into our two families, but that wasn't enough. I needed to get out."

The change-in-priorities marriage

Simone and Brenhan were a great couple for eighteen years. They had met at the University of Paris when they were both nineteen and Brenhan was in France on a student-exchange program. They fell in love and she came back to the States to live with him. He went on to the diplomatic corps, and she developed a talent in public relations. They were an attractive couple who dressed beautifully and went to glamorous parties. It suited them both extremely well until Simone, at thirty-seven, realized that, more than anything in her life, she wanted a child. And she needed to act right away because time was her enemy. She had gone to a doctor and determined that having a baby was still possible. She had been bringing the issue up for several years now, rather gingerly because she knew Brenhan liked his lifestyle, which involved a lot of travel and the ability to take off at a moment's notice. He had always said "Maybe later," but now that she realized this was a number-one priority, she said that the time had to be this year. She was shocked and furious when he said that he had thought about it and decided he just couldn't have a child: It would ruin his life, and, he thought, it would ruin their marriage. He loved having her all to himself. He watched their friends change when they had kids and, frankly, he didn't like what he saw. The answer was no.

This sent Simone into a tailspin. She realized that she had been kidding herself about how Brenhan really felt and that if she wanted a child she would have to leave the marriage. She went into counseling for two years and, at the end of it, she told Brenhan she was leaving him. He was upset, he did not want her to leave, but he was just as passionate about not wanting a child as she was passionate about having one. And so he let her go.

Simone was extremely unhappy for a about a year and waffled back and forth about going back to Brenhan. It had been a good marriage and she missed him. But at the end of the year she met Jason, an account executive in an advertising firm and a man who had just left a marriage with a similar problem, except in his case, he was the person who wanted children. It was a huge bond between them, and they became intimate talking about their individual agony over separation and why children were so important. Jason was about four years younger than Simone and not in quite the same hurry. But he knew how important having a child was for her, so after they decided they were in love, they tried to conceive a baby. She was four months pregnant when they got married. Divorce for Simone was absolutely necessary. Her first marriage wasn't unsuccessful; it was just wrapped around priorities that she didn't share. The marriage just didn't fulfill her priority, and I think she was smart to be disciplined and insistent about what she needed.

The child-raising marriage

Dina and Brewster were married for thirty years. They raised four children, and they did it beautifully. Each one of their children had a happy childhood, and each went on to a good job or higher education. They loved almost everything about being a family and although they knew it would be a big change when the last child left home at nineteen to go to school, they hadn't expected it to feel as if someone had let the air out their tires. But it did.

They tried to ignore the gap between them. They both got into hobbies. He, golf, gardening, and driving downstate to go to every one of his daughter's golf competitions. Dina spent even more time with her friends, intensified her commitment to deaf children, and became absorbed in overseeing the new, smaller house they were building. But the truth hit them hard when they went on a long-awaited cruise to Latin America and it was clear that they were not having as good a time as they wanted to. In fact, one night after dinner, while they were sitting in their stateroom, Dina brought up the obvious and asked why they were staying together now.

They both felt so guilty. They liked each other. They were proud of what they had done. But somehow, somewhere along the way, they had lost each other as favorite companions and they couldn't seem to get the feeling back. They went to therapy and took a good look at their situation. But after about five sessions, they both agreed to call it quits. Friends were shocked and could not believe that things were as amicable as they seemed. Neither was involved with anyone else, nor was there great anger or accusations. As Dina said, "Sometimes a marriage just runs out of steam, and I suppose Brewster and I were unusual enough to acknowledge it and do something about it. I know we will always be friends. And I think that is better for us now than trying to pretend that we are also lovers. When we tried to be husband and wife it seemed false. Friends seems right. The kids are quite upset, of course, but they are coming around. And I think Brewster and I are both doing fine."

♥

Marriages do cool off. That's fine if a cool, comfortable, disengaged home life seems about right—which it does to a lot of couples. For some, friendship is enough after a while; but others don't want the second twenty-five years to be any different from the first. Why not recognize the tenor of the relationship and if there is not more growth or change in it, end it rather than just stay roommates?

Some relationships just outlive their purpose, and that's a fact. But if you are married or cohabiting or in a long-term same-sex relationship, almost everyone you know will tell you to stay anyhow. If there are children, the pressure will be enormous. I'm not saying that there might not be stronger arguments to stay than to leave, but sometimes leaving is the right thing to do. Some relationships were meant to have existed and meant to end (we won't even dignify by mentioning them ones that were mistakes from the beginning). Here are some of the arguments detractors will use, and while they may all have some truth to them, I'm here to poke a few holes in their logic.

You are being selfish

Maybe you are, but sometimes that's a good thing and your selfishness might protect you. Even if there are small children, who is to say that they will not be better off if you are happier. I know there are many circumstances in which it is best to stay for the children—maybe most. But it certainly isn't good if you are in a high-conflict relationship or if you are depressed. Or if it means spending your life feeling unloved or being unloving.

But why not be selfish? Whom are you living your life for, yourself or your neighbors, family, and friends? Are they living inside your skin and soul? We are meant to be selfish animals; otherwise we wouldn't survive. Of course, we are also meant to be generous and affiliated— that helps us survive as well. The point is finding a balance, and only you can know where that balance is and what makes sense. Just don't let the "selfish" epithet undo you when it is inevitably thrown at you. Everyone is selfish in his or her own way—other people's version of self-interest might just not be so public. Surely you owe it to your relationship to try hard to make it work, but ultimately it has to work for both of you.

You owe it to your children

Of course you owe a lot to your children. You owe them your loyalty, advice, love, resources, presence—we could put together a list we would all agree on. But do you owe them your entire emotional fulfillment? Is that really what is required? I guess I am a typical baby boomer. It's not that I don't believe in home and family and taking care of children. Of course I do. But I know that personal happiness should weigh in on this list. And the question is, How much does your relationship affect it?

This is a real question because some people can do quite well in a relationship that is effectively without love, sex, or emotional intimacy. They get those things outside the marriage, or they do well enough without them. They are satisfied with having some company, joint resources, and another parent for their children. If this is what makes you happy, or happy enough, then by all means stay with a relationship and protect your interests.

But for some people, their day-to-day happiness is continually affected by whether or not they have a partner whom they are loved by and in love with. Even these people may not need passion, but they need a sense of not being emotionally alone. And without this feeling, their lives are increasingly lonely and depressing. What price should these people pay for their children's welfare?

The answer is something well-meaning people can and do differ on. There is certainly a cacophony of voices that, after viewing some of the carnage of divorce—impoverished women, children deserted by fathers or neglected by overwhelmed mothers—support the family's staying together *no matter what*. That may be the choice that is best for many families and most children. But you, as the only one who will live your life and make the judgments about what can be done to safeguard your kids, are entitled to make your own choice. And for some people, this has got to be for a better emotional match. Sometimes the kids actually understand what is wrong and are supportive of separation. Children are not always against divorce, no matter what the books tell you.

You will get through this and be happy in your old age

Well, how old are you now? And how long do you want to wait? It's true that things may be better in your old age, but it is also true that they may not. One of the things my mom said to me that always has rung true is that "when people get older, they just get more so." By which she meant that there was an intensification of who they were, not a change. If you don't like your partner now, the chances are that when you get older you will want to kill him. And that, sadly enough, is something adult children with aging parents often actually worry about. The end of the life cycle, if it goes into the late seventies, eighties, and nineties, is often not a pretty sight. Even without the varying debilitating physical and mental illnesses that commonly arise, there is also a certain amount of crankiness and marital discord between parents that breaks adult children's hearts. There is no guarantee that you will turn into a beautiful old couple who will be photographed snuggling at ninety. Rather, there is every chance that if you aren't too happy together now, when you are eighty-seven your children will be answering your incessant calls complaining about your spouse and asking why you can't live with them.

You will never find anyone else

If you are a woman, your friends will shake their heads knowingly and tell you to hang on to what you've got. They will quote statistics and tell you that if you leave you won't find anyone else and that if you do, he won't be any better than the one you've got. (Men don't get the same advice. On the contrary, they are told about how quickly they will get snapped up, which is true. They are, however, a little scared about who will do the snapping.)

However slim the pickings may be after forty or so, remarriage or re-coupling is still possible. It just depends on how committed you are to finding someone and how good you feel about yourself. In my experience, women who are self-confident, happy people and who really get themselves out there into the social mix, find someone. They may not remarry (they may not want to), but life surprises them with just as much interesting experience as they had before. This is true for both straight and gay women. I have a good friend who at sixty thought her life was winding down. Since then, however, she had a serious several-year love affair with the "love of her life" and became CEO of a company. Life was hardly over. Now, I'm not saying that's a typical story. If anyone leaves a relationship, she should be prepared to be alone for a while. It takes time to get over the end of a relationship, and remembering how to be alone and figuring out how you want to reconstitute your life takes some time. Jumping into a new relationship right away has its own problems. Second marriages also have a high divorce rate, and putting together a new life when both people have complex lives isn't simple. Still, I am also saying that I know of more success stories than of regrets.

For example, I know a woman, Tiki, who at thirty left her first husband because he was very controlling and resented the demands of her career. She started a jewelry business and handsomely supported her two daughters from her first marriage. Then she met a man who she admits was "a temporary solace" and not a good lifetime choice, and they were married for about five years and had twins. He drank and grew morose and she hated to admit she had made a bad mistake, but she did and sued for divorce. At thirty-seven she was dating and moved in with a man, a wealthy businessman ten years her senior, but again she found him overbearing and she left, four children in tow. She dated around and finally, at forty-five, met Ari, a Greek businessman/lawyer whose first wife had died. He was the father of two sons, both off to college. The two of them have been together for ten years, completely comfortable and happy.

Tiki was never alone for any appreciable time. A talented, successful, warm, and sociable person, she simply put herself out in the world, and adventure and suitors appeared periodically. She never worried; she always assumed she would pair up. It is not only lovely and talented women who find a way to be happy and not alone. A good social life is a product of attitude, not a perfect face or figure (though certainly these help).

You can't escape angst, so stay put. If you leave, you will just bring yourself with you

This school of thought tells you that it's always your fault. It says it's not the relationship, and if you leave you will be the same person in the next one. Unless you have been in four marriages and left them all furiously mad at the other person's faults, I wouldn't believe this. (and research supports me: most people do not divorce the second time over the same issues present in their first marriage.) Unless you are highly neurotic (and I hope you know if you are or not), you are a different person under new conditions and with a new person. Of course there will be some consistencies, but all people are not the same and you are not the same with them. Otherwise you could have married anyone, right?

You have a perfectly good relationship

They may be right. No one is telling you ever to leave a relationship lightly, especially one that has been a success in some ways. But only you can decide if it's good enough to be in for a lifetime. No one else can have your perspective. Remember that when you listen to other people's advice. People tend to be conservative, that is, they want to conserve what is. But you may know that the successful part of your relationship is over and what is left is not going to be uplifting to your spirit or your spouse's. The myth that society will use against you is this: If you leave, it will be a "failed marriage or relationship," and you will be at fault. But you know that it is already a "failed marriage" and staying will not make it succeed. The pressure to ignore that fact will be enormous. But if you know that the marriage or cohabitation has no more growth or comfort or function in it, you can move on. The past can be respected, perhaps celebrated, even as the future beckons.

24

MYTH:
Children bring a couple closer

If I were to pick the top myth out of the twenty-five I have as-
sembled, the one that has done the most damage to the most
people would be this one. It's not that children aren't wonderful;
of course they are. And it's not that we shouldn't have them—it's hard
for me to imagine my life without having had my kids. But people
really need to know the truth about kids and love, romance and marriage, and the truth is that if your love affair survives having kids, you
have achieved a minor miracle. Am I being too dramatic? I really don't
think so. People who think that a new baby will fix any of their relationship angst find out that the result is almost always that children
complicate the relationship and make it more difficult. Partners' fantasy
about child-raising is that children will increase love and intimacy, but
their fantasy rarely includes worry, fatigue, issues over participation,
and loss of privacy and time for each other. Let's take a look at the
myths and then the realities.

Having a child is the most intimate thing that can happen between a man and a woman

Actually I think that the most intimate thing that can happen between a man and a woman is voluntarily to choose to have a child together and have sex knowing that you are trying to create a child. That is romantic, intense, wonderful. I'd even say that being pregnant with someone who loves you and is committed to being with you forever is very intimate and wonderful. Many men, and most women, are fascinated with the changes that occur as the baby grows and thrives. However, this is also the moment for some couples when intimacy starts to diverge according to how either a man or a woman feels about pregnancy. If she feels unattractive or sick, she may start shutting him out. She doesn't want to be touched, much less made love to. She just wants to get through this.

Elise, for example, voiced a common story: "I felt like a cow, and there was nothing that T.K. could say or do that would make me feel better. He would tell me how beautiful I looked and I thought it was a nice effort—but that was all. I didn't like to make love. I just felt uncomfortable and bloated. I either said no or just kind of lay there waiting for him to get it over with. Pretty soon he stopped asking, and I was relieved."

This is quite common. I have done a column for *American Baby* magazine for many years and spoken in person to many audiences of young mothers. While some of them have a surge of sexual interest in the second trimester, far more of them find that at some point of the pregnancy cycle, they would just prefer to forget about sex and any kind of physical intimacy. But let's say the wife is fine. In fact, pregnancy has made her super horny (it happens!). Then the question is, Does her body turn him on? Sometimes, it does, and pregnancy turns into a pretty sexy time for both of them. But many wives feel that their body is not what their husband wants and that it is his, not their own, sex drive that diminishes. Men worry that intercourse will hurt the baby (even if she tells them that her doctor said that shouldn't be a concern), or they just think of her in maternal rather than sexual terms. They may still be affectionate, but not really turned-on.

So does it get better when the child is born? If you have had a child, most of you know the answer to that is no. In fact, for many couples, not only their sex life but also their emotional intimacy steadily unravels. This is an outcome of a common problem: absorption of the woman in the role of mother. Most women just go bananas for their new child. They are in love—madly, passionately in love. But, they are also worried. There are a dozen little things a day that make them worried—the baby isn't eating, the baby is having trouble breast-feeding, the baby is having trouble pooping, the baby has a temperature—you name it. They are worried, and they are tired. While some babies have read the good-baby book and start sleeping five hours a night or more, most babies are up at random times throughout the night. If a woman has the total participation of her husband, she will be less fatigued; but even if he is helping a lot, the best they can hope for is that both of them are tired—she just somewhat less so than if she were doing all this by herself.

Guess what anxiety and intense love and fatigue add up to? Rare sex and, sometimes, not even emotional attention. This is the stage of a marriage where there is a chance for a triangle to develop (mother-child-father). And triangles are an inherently unstable constructions. People tend to team up and, in this case, the likeliest team is going to be mother and child with Dad being odd man out. Many men understand that this is going to happen for a while, and they may be understanding and supportive. But even the most understanding man starts to get angry, jealous, and competitive if this goes on for more than six months. Some men don't have that much patience, and they start getting jealous and resentful right away. Not much of this adds up to intimacy (unless the couple follows some of the rules I am going to give later in this chapter).

Well, of course your sex life suffers for a while, but that will not continue to be a problem after a few months

That's not the way I see the data. Unless a couple really works hard to make it otherwise, a lot of patterns begin at this time that seem to be hard to break. Men get used to leaving their wives alone, and women get their love and affection and even physical pleasure (in a way) from their child. As one mother said to me on a television show in Seattle, "I get sucked on and handled by my child all day. I don't want to be sucked on and pulled on at night as well!" It is amazing to me how frequently young mothers express their distaste for further physical activity.

And this can last for a long time. Even if sex happens, either one or both partners are usually distracted. One ear is perked toward the baby, or maybe the toddler might open the door crying. I don't know how common it is for couples to have the baby in bed with them or in their room—but, from anecdotal stories, it seems very ordinary. In fact, what is amazing is how long couples will allow their child to sleep in their room, sometimes even after the child has entered kindergarten! If a child insists on being part of the family bedroom, one or both parents usually give in. They are afraid that denying the child access will hurt the child in some way. There is certainly no evidence for this, but there is plenty of evidence that if the adults are never alone in their own bedroom, adult sexual and verbal intimacy will be affected negatively. There are a lot of marriages that start to go sideways even if one of the people in the relationship is totally unaware that this is happening. For example, June is a bright, beautiful lawyer who was married to a television executive. Juggling both a demanding career and new motherhood, she accepted the fact that she and her husband were so absorbed in their individual lives and baby caretaking that their intimacy had temporarily (she thought) evaporated. Sex had become infrequent to nonexistent, and they had stopped dancing and socializing the way they had before the baby came. She figured that sooner or later they would get around repairing the damage once he stopped traveling so much and the baby was old enough to go to preschool. But she never got that chance. When the baby was eighteen months old, her husband came home one night and announced that he was in love with someone else—that he had felt lonely and abandoned during her pregnancy and that he had been having an affair that turned into a love relationship when the baby was six months old and he was leaving. He did, leaving her flabbergasted and hugely hurt. When she looks back on it now, some years later and just remarried herself, she sees how their marriage began to be devitalized during the period of pregnancy and infancy, but she had thought that was par for the course. She still hated him for leaving her when he did and the way he did, but she admitted that they both had some responsibility for letting the relationship get sour.

♥

The new baby makes all this seem necessary, but it really isn't. This is not a time for shutting a partner out, no matter how difficult incorporating anyone else into this tiny circle seems to be. Couples need to find private, intimate time, even if it's only for a two-hour dinner out, so they can be focused on just the two of them. Better yet, get a sitter or friend or relative to take care of the baby while you run out for romantic night at a hotel or borrowed apartment for a quick tryst. Lovemaking and intimate discussion should not be back-burnered for too long or the relationship may go from cool to cold.

Okay, so taking time for each other is hard when the child is an infant, but things go back to where they were once the child is a little older

It's amazing how long these patterns can go on. Mothers often feel they can never leave their child alone, no matter how old he or she is. It is not uncommon for couples to go for five years or more without taking a vacation, even a night, without their child. This doesn't even depend on whether or not they have good child care (although of course not having access to child care complicates the picture enormously). Sometimes women just can't bear to leave their children even for a day.

When the child enters kindergarten or day care, these patterns may have become so entrenched that the couple stays on a parallel tract— she busying herself with kid-related activities, he being the after-work father or weekend dad. If they try to share behaviors by syncopating their schedule, each person does get relief time, but no intimacy time together. This can stretch on for years and years.

Well, maybe it's hard when the kids need so much of the mother's time, but once they are in middle school or high school you get a lot of time back for each other

If a couple thinks managing babyhood is demanding, think of handling adolescence as the Ph.D. exams for matrimony. Adolescents these days are beginning their own sexual lives, and the issues their sexuality and their desire for independence bring up are often very hard on the parents unless they have complete consensus about how to handle these challenges. A husband or a wife, or both, may feel threatened by a child who has different ethical or moral guidelines than they do and clamp down on the child's privacy and freedom. The young person can resist, doing everything from dying his hair purple, to staying out all night without permission, to flaunting his sexual experience. A child's truculent attitude or disrespectful mouth can not only stir up a parent's anger at the child; it can also set parent against parent as they react differently to different provocations. Maintaining solidarity, much less intimacy, is no small accomplishment. A lot of parents just can't do it.

It's just so easy to get on the opposite side from one another when it comes to children. For example, Peg and Toby had a wonderful early marriage together. They met in beauty school and worked together, partied together, and ultimately married and chipped in to start their own salon. They really had a great time until they had kids. "Then," says Toby, "I lost my wife. She got conservative, wanted me home early, dropped out of the salon, and got really uninterested in it altogether. She became really interested in the PTA, and she basically turned into another person. She thinks I'm an authority freak and a shit, and I think she would let them pee on the carpets if they wanted to. We don't agree on anything with them, and sometimes its just stone-cold in that house. I'm unhappy a lot of the time— she rarely wants to make love with me anymore—in fact, she told me that she rarely ever misses it. I've thought of an affair, but I'm not that kind of guy. And I don't want to risk losing my kids. But I feel that I got lied to—about who she was. I don't know how this happened to us."

♥

What can you do about it? It is so easy to let kids get in the middle of the relationship, but it is avoidable. First, though, you have to get over the idea that just because you both want and love children, they will necessarily bring you together. Here's some practical advice.

Don't be drawn off into parallel worlds

It may be good for your career to do split-shift caretaking, or it may maximize income if one person takes on all the child care and the other is free to be as ambitious and career oriented as possible. But after a while, partners are living in parallel worlds and that creates distance, not intimacy. Dads who really pitch in are very much appreciated by most wives if they pitch in early enough, and the mother doesn't start to think of the children as her wholly owned property and expertise. The more that is shared from pregnancy on, the more likely it is to add to the relationship. Sure, you can start just thinking of each other as Mom and Dad if you don't leaven your mutual child raising with some romance. And if you don't agree on most child-raising policies, togetherness can just cause more conflict over the kids. Still, most of the time, taking care of kids together creates a strong, affectionate bond.

Don't let your child take you away from each other

Children want to be the center of attention. They need a lot from you, and they will take most of what you have to give and then say it's not enough. Most working parents feel guilty that they are not giving their children the time they need, so they take all their spare time and make it family time instead of couple time. But you need couple time, and sometimes family time just won't do. It may be great to go on a family picnic, but it isn't going to be the same as a picnic with you and your sweetie. You may think you are getting enough time together if you are with your partner and your child, but it is never going to be as romantic as it could be alone, and the chance of having meaningful conversations is low. Have a date at least once a week, a romantic getaway at least once a month. Right from the beginning.

Become yourself again as soon as you can

Remember who you were when your partner fell in love with you. Were you slim and athletic? Randy and flirtatious? Always planning inventive getaways or doing activities together? Whatever it is, don't lose it. Sometimes we have this myth that our soul is what our partner is supposed to love, no matter what, and the package and accoutrements shouldn't matter. Maybe ideally that is true, but real life is something different. Remember: You fell in love with each other as lovers and friends, not parents. Don't let the parent persona take over. Don't give up passion, attractiveness, and sexuality because you think your job now is to be family member rather than a romantic partner.

Don't let children come between you

If you have radically different approaches to your kids or even in terms of planning for them, nip the coming conflict in the bud and get counseling. Everyone has strong feelings about their children, and letting these differences fester and remain unresolved can result in an explosive or nasty situation that can blow the relationship apart. Even if the relationship remains intact, you don't want to spend all your child-rearing years at home butting heads about how they are raised. Remember, anger is the biggest enemy of sex and intimacy there is, and conflict over kids is a common source of that anger. Don't let it tear your relationship apart. Plan ahead, or if it's too late for that, get help.

Address any problems, sexual or otherwise, right away

It's difficult to confront your partner—most of us would rather wait and hope that problems will go away all by themselves. But mostly they don't. Psychologists will tell you that the couples who are the most fragile are not the ones who argue—arguing is okay, it gets stuff out in the open. No, the couples who get in trouble are the ones who never *solve* anything. Issues crop up but never get handled. And eventually so much anger and resentment gets built up that those emotions are harder to solve than the original issue. Whatever it is—help with the baby, time with each other, or differences about child raising—face it when it happens and deal with it.

25

MYTH:
Committed and married people should live in the same home

A mong the assumptions we make, living together is so taken for granted that we don't even imagine another way of doing it. But if you think about it, people really do vary their living arrangements when they need to. We all know commuting couples who are stuck in separate cities for a while or dating couples who keep separate apartments even though they spend almost every night together. Still, the presumption is that if couples could live together, they would—and they should. I am not arguing that everyone should have separate homes; too many people would be lonely—and poorer! But there are some circumstances that beg for separate living arrangements and I think many couples would be far happier, in fact less likely to break up, if they felt free to have separate places.

The most common model for this is among older couples. Fran, a fifty-nine-year-old woman writer was married when she was in her twenties and early thirties. Then, when her marriage broke up, she lived with her children until they went off to college and, ultimately, to lives of their own. From her forties on, she lived alone, and while she would have very much liked to have found another steady partner, she never did. She gave up on having more than an occasional lover now and then and when she first met Warren, she assumed that he too would be a passing flirtation.

They met in Pacific Heights, a densely populated part of San Francisco where they both lived, while they were walking their dogs. After weeks of casually acknowledging each other's presence, they started talking. He worked in the public relations office of one of the local theaters, and it turned out they had some mutual acquaintances. They became more friendly and she found out that he was divorced, also had adult children, and was just a little bit older than she was. He was attractive and kind, and finally she worked up the nerve to ask him over for a glass of wine.

They had a good time that night, and he started to come over almost nightly. Eventually he ended up spending the night. They started walking their dogs together regularly and spending a lot of time over at each other's apartments. "But it surprised me," said Fran, "that I really didn't want to move in with him, or vice versa. I liked the fact that he lived across the street, that we could retreat back to our own little spaces, that there would still be a place for me to unwind, pig out, whatever it is that I do."

Warren was relieved that Fran felt this way. He had had a really ugly divorce, his ex-wife was mentally unstable, called incessantly, and turned up suddenly and sometimes acted violently. He felt that he didn't have the right or desire to expose someone else to the troubles she caused in his life. At first he thought that Fran would pressure him or that maybe he should pressure himself. "I wondered if it was a sign that I didn't love Fran because I didn't want to move in with her or have her move in with me. But then I began to think—no, it doesn't have to be that way. We are mature adults and we can do this any damn way we please."

And indeed, that is the way it has gone for years. Fran thinks they would have broken up long ago if they had organized their lives any other way. "He has so much craziness in his life. He's got this son in trouble, a wife who is dangerous, a business that is a pressure cooker—things I don't think I can take on anymore. But he is a dear sweet man, a wonderful lover, and I love him. So this way we can have the best of each other and I can still go home and have the time I need there."

♥

I know of quite a few stories that are variations on this theme. Two perfectly good people love each other, but there are parts of each other's lives that would scuttle their relationship if they were forced to put their entire households together. Most couples cannot resist the desire to live together, so if the rest of the baggage they carry is lethal—they let it pollute the relationship. But there is a choice for most, though not all, couples (this would be very hard, and unfair, to do if you had small children together). For couples who are pre– or post–child-raising, however, there is really some possibility that it could allow a relationship that had many strengths, but some important deficits, to flourish.

For example, Samantha and John are both artists. Samantha is a composer and John is a painter. They both like space that is their own. They don't want anything touched, much less moved. They found that living together, they were always in each other's way—never getting the uninterrupted solitude they needed to do their artistic work. They were getting on each other's nerves and wondering about whether or not the relationship was going to work when an apartment became available directly across from the apartment they lived in together. One of them, neither of them can remember who, mused semi-seriously about how great it would be if they rented the other apartment and then visited each other's place at night. Then they started to seriously discuss it. And then they did it. They have loved this arrangement, which has gone for several years now. They are very happy with each other, look forward to their visits, and feel that they have just the right amount of intimacy and privacy. Samantha says, "I think it was the psychologist Fritz Perls, who said, 'If you love something, set it free.' I always thought that was a little glib, but it makes sense to me now. We didn't work well together when we felt constrained. And we did feel boxed in when we had to share space for everything. We were walking on eggshells around each other, and it was destructive. Once we could give each other creative and physical space, it was like there was more oxygen between us. So I think it is true that freedom gave us the ability to become closer."

♥

This answer can't be for everyone, but it is a good idea for some people. The question to think about is, When, if ever, would it be the right thing for you to do?

When you (or your partner) have lived alone a long time and you are pretty inflexible about compromise

If people have lived alone for a long time, they often get set in their own routines and for some people, this has a sacred quality and they just cannot change. I have known people who do not want to talk, literally, before they have their tea and read their paper. One man I know takes an hour and half to shower, shave, and do a few exercises in the morning and said that it drove his ex-wife crazy. They only had one small bathroom, and he was always in her way. One of the consolations of the divorce, he reported, was that he was delighted to have his very own bathroom all to himself.

These may sound like small things, and to some people they are. But there are people, and you may be one of them, who treasure privacy, routine, silence, and other personal pleasures so much that they find do not blend well with other people in the household. Once they have what they need, they are perfectly personable—but if they get interrupted or diverted they can be beastly. If they have the time and the privacy to have these small rituals, they feel that the world is in order— if they don't, they are resentful. If you or your partner just can't have someone at the sink with you, never wants to see the toilet seat up (or down), why hassle over it? Meet after the coffee has been drunk, the hot water is gone—and you are ready to be human again.

When you have children from another marriage and your partner doesn't get along with them well, or vice versa

There is a higher divorce rate in second marriages than first marriages, and research suggests that the higher rate is almost entirely attributable to having children from a previous marriage present. Kids are hard enough to raise when they are your own. When they are someone else's, the issues—from the cost of the child to the child's resentment of the new parent to the child's difficulty getting along at school (or with law-enforcement authorities)—can be more stress than the second marriage can take. Some people parent extremely well together, and they figure out a way to keep the child or children from hurting the marriage, but more people than expected it have seen their marriages torn apart because of disagreements or turmoil caused by stepchildren who grew up in a different family culture. While it is natural for the custodial parent to want her new partner to help her give her child a better life, it is not a bad idea to make a clear-eyed assessment about how this new family system will fit together. And, if the fit looks really bad, or starts to feel really bad, imagine a living arrangement that might take some of the pressure off—and let more days be good days together. Unusual? Yes. Constructive? Yes, and maybe relationship saving.

♥   *271*

When you love each other but come from "different lives"

There are people you fall in love with who are so different from you that none of your friends mesh, your tastes in furniture and housing are totally different, and your habits (like going to bars or ballet) contradict each other. Still, you are terrific together if you pick the right place, and if you don't put in these other jarring elements that aren't complementary you have more intimacy and fun than you've ever had with anyone else. But when you try to force it to be a complete package, the fact that you have lived different lives becomes too apparent and it forces you to back away from one another.

Why break up over furniture? Why not see your friends in your own home and never have to force them, or your partner, to suffer the mismatch? You can keep a coherent lifestyle separately, visit each other's world happily—but not have to live there. For example, I knew a woman who was in love with a horse trainer. He lived in a cramped trailer at the track he worked at because he needed to be near his horses. When he wasn't there, he was at another trailer at a breeding farm where he worked, being near the mares at foaling time or staying there overnight because it was convenient since his day began so early. The trailer was grungy and she didn't like staying there; it "depressed" her. Likewise, he found her condo "confining" and too "white." While he was fastidious with his bridles and saddles he was, to put it mildly, casual about order in his own household. Still, this couple had a lot in common. They were both environmentalists and outdoors people. They both loved animals. They had a great sex life, and just about everything worked, except they felt much more comfortable in their own space than in each other's, so they both kept their own place—and it worked for a long time. Eventually, they had a serious talk about the future and realized they wanted more time together—but still couldn't imagine sharing the same space. So they bought land and built two small houses on the same property, back to back but separate. He still spends time in trailers when he thinks he has to, but they preserved both their separation and their intimate and committed relationship.

When you are a person who needs solitude to get back to feeling in balance

As I mentioned earlier, the first category of the Meyers-Briggs psychological test measures people on whether or not they are an introvert or an extrovert. The designers of the psychological profile test are not just testing whether or not a person likes to be around people. Rather, they are looking at different dimensions: where a person draws his strength from; if he is facing a challenge, does he go to a friend or draw a team of people together? Or does he seek solitude, concentrate, and then come up with a solution from within himself? In other words, is he a person who seeks his own counsel, or does he seek it from others? If you do the former, you measure as an introvert; the latter, an extrovert. Introverts, at least under this definition, often need a place to be alone that can help restore them to where they need to be. A shared home may work fine as long as there are private spaces and private time. But for some people, that is not enough. They need their own truly separate environment; but that doesn't mean they don't want a truly close relationship at other times. If you are an introvert on the Meyers-Briggs, you might be the kind of person who keeps a place of your own, as well as shares space with someone else. You might like to be very present when you want to be and gone when you need to be. At least, it's worth thinking about.

In truth, few young couples will take this option. There is such a great need for most people to be with their partner all the time, to crawl inside a bed together every night, and to share time in the precious few unencumbered moments that are available. But older couples, particularly people who have been married a long time, divorced, and spent a lot of time on their own, should at least think about the possibility that staying apart will keep you together for a much longer time.

Some concluding remarks

There are a lot of myths, or at least half-truths, about love and sex. I can think of many others to talk about, and maybe I will in a follow-up book. But right now, those discussed in the preceding chapters are the ones that I feel mislead people in significant ways. But of course, within every list is an inner list, the top criminals in a list of dangerous characters. So since we all have minuscule attention spans, let me remind you of five important points:

1. Beware the myth that kids bring you together

I have already tipped you off on this one because I think it is so important. People who have not had a child—and even people who have—have no idea how hard kids are on sexuality and romance. People should have children because they love them and need them and want to help create the future of the world. But don't think it isn't a sacrifice for the relationship. It's the biggest one you will make. You will gain immensely by having children, but be prepared to lose something between you for a while—or, if you aren't careful, forever.

2. Take a good look at the norms and values of cohabitation

Short term, no problem. Long term, it's every man and woman for him- or herself. I think long-term cohabitation makes us less generous toward each other—something I think has serious costs for our relationships, and for our ability to be good partners.

3. The past predicts the present

Several of these myths posit that someone will be a new, changed person just because he or she has met you. Don't believe it. Sexuality, values, and habits *can* change because of a new relationship, but most of the time you should be prepared to get more of the same. We all hope to change the parts of someone that are less palatable to us—but we shouldn't pin our hopes on it. If someone has something about her or him that you don't love, accept it or go elsewhere.

4. Compromise is "necessary"

On the other hand, there is no need to lose the very things that you once prized most about life just because you've fallen in love. I hate the myth that sets people up to cheat themselves of what is most meaningful to them. If you love someone and he or she loves you, then you should help each other not to be deflected from your most important dreams.

5. Consider when to fight, and when not to fight

So much of creating a successful relationship is knowing when to back off and then actually doing it. I think I could write a whole book about the things we know we shouldn't do—yet we do anyway because we want to resolve our anxiety as soon as possible. In the case of fights, backing off for a while is essential. If more of us would do it, some fights wouldn't happen at all—and the ones that do would happen when we are better prepared, more rational, and feeling less cornered. We'd fight better, cleaner, and probably achieve more lasting solutions. If that isn't important in long-term relationships, I don't know what is.

♥

And that brings up a final caveat. All of us are more expert about someone else's life than we are about our own. We can know a solid principle, and still it is hard to apply it when we need to. No matter how savvy or expert we are in general about life, it is impossible to be perfectly wise about love or sex or commitment. There is so much to be wrong about! There is so much interference from our hormones and our fantasies! We need each other's intuitions, observations, and knowledge to muddle through and maybe, just maybe, find someone, keep someone, and be happy. I hope that this book has given you some additional insights that will help you tailor your love life to your needs and personality, rather than continuing to depend on some cultural habits or ideologies that might not suit you—and in fact, really suit very few people. We need to be original thinkers in the twenty-first century. Love and sexuality are important to most of us, and a little hardheaded thinking about these softest, most heartfelt of topics might just help us all have a better chance of intimacy in the years ahead.